DK EYEWITNESS

DOMINICAN REPUBLIC

JAMES FERGUSON

DK

Left **Windsurfing, Cabarete** Center **Church, La Romana** Right **Victorian houses, Malecón**

LONDON, NEW YORK,
MELBOURNE, MUNICH AND DELHI
www.dk.com

Reproduced by Colourscan, Singapore
Printed and bound in Italy by Graphicom

First American Edition, 2005
05 06 07 08 09 10 9 8 7 6

Published in the United States by
DK Publishing, Inc.,
375 Hudson Street
New York, New York 10014

ISSN 1479-344X
ISBN 0-7566-0904-6

Within each Top 10 list in this book, no
hierarchy of quality or popularity is
implied. All 10 are, in the editor's
opinion, of roughly equal merit.

Contents

Dominican Republic's Top 10

Left **San Juan de la Maguana statue** Center **Playa El Macao** Right **Calle del Sol, Santiago**

Left **Exhibits outside Museo de Arte, Bonao** Right **Boaters near El Morro**

Key to abbreviations
Adm admission charge **Free** no admission charge **Dis. access** disabled access

3

DOMINICAN REPUBLIC'S TOP 10

DOMINICAN REPUBLIC'S TOP 10

TOP 10 Dominican Republic Highlights

The Dominican Republic is a country of surprising contrasts and extraordinary variety. From the chilly peak of the Caribbean's highest mountain to some of the region's most delightful beaches, the country boasts lush valleys, spectacular waterfalls, and sun-baked deserts. The past and present also blend in a fascinating mix of colonial buildings and modern hotels, sleepy rural villages and lively tourist resorts. The people, too, reflect a kaleidoscope of influences – Spanish, African, indigenous – creating a culture that emphasizes both creativity and fun in the fields of music, sport, and art.

1 Santo Domingo: The Zona Colonial

The historic jewel in the capital's crown, this district of restored colonial buildings and shady plazas is filled with well-preserved reminders of a bygone age (see pp8–9).

2 Santo Domingo: The Modern City

The modern metropolis encompasses crowded downtown streets, charming suburbs, and relaxing parks, where art galleries rub shoulders with US-style shopping malls (see pp10–11).

3 Constanza & "The Dominican Alps"

Only two hours from the capital, the rugged interior is a walker's paradise of green meadows and clear rivers, surrounded by pine forests and mountains. Pico Duarte, the highest mountain in the Caribbean, lies here (see pp12–13).

4 Santiago

The laid-back second city is different in ambience from bustling Santo Domingo. Its streets are filled with monuments to its past glories as a tobacco boom town (see pp14–15).

Map labels: La Isabela Bay 6 · Luperón · Puerto Plata 5 · Monte Cristi · Dajabón · Mao · Esperanza · Sabaneta · Santiago 4 · HAITI · San José de las Matas · La Vega · Jarabacoa · Pico Duarte 3087m · Parque Nacional Jose del Carmen Ramirez · Cons 3 · Las Matas de Farfán · San Juan de la Maguana · Lago Enriquillo 10 · Neiba · Fondo Negro · San José de Ocoa · Cabral · Azua · Parque Nacional Sierra de Baoruco · Barahona · Pedernales · Baoruco · Valle del Cibao · Cordillera · Central · Yaque del Norte · miles 0 km 50

Previous pages **Archway in Santo Domingo**

Puerto Plata
5 Steeped in colonial history, the North Coast port is also the hub for the area's thriving tourist complexes, offering a great combination of sightseeing and entertainment. Tourist attractions include the San Felipe Fortress, La Glorieta, and Museo del Ambar *(see pp16–17)*.

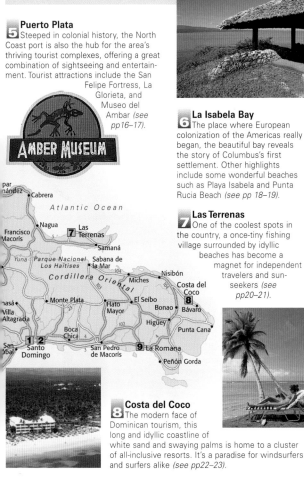

AMBER MUSEUM

La Isabela Bay
6 The place where European colonization of the Americas really began, the beautiful bay reveals the story of Columbus's first settlement. Other highlights include some wonderful beaches such as Playa Isabela and Punta Rucia Beach *(see pp 18–19)*.

Las Terrenas
7 One of the coolest spots in the country, a once-tiny fishing village surrounded by idyllic beaches has become a magnet for independent travelers and sun-seekers *(see pp20–21)*.

Costa del Coco
8 The modern face of Dominican tourism, this long and idyllic coastline of white sand and swaying palms is home to a cluster of all-inclusive resorts. It's a paradise for windsurfers and surfers alike *(see pp22–23)*.

La Romana
9 A town built on sugar now offers a different sweetness in the form of the country's most luxurious resort, Casa de Campo, and an unforgettable transplant from Italy, Altos de Chavón *(see pp24–25)*.

Lago Enriquillo
10 An inland saltwater sea surrounded by cactus-studded wilderness, this natural wonder involves a boat trip and close encounters with crocodiles and tame giant iguanas *(see pp26–27)*.

Dominican Republic's Top 10

🔟 Santo Domingo: The Zona Colonial

The Zona Colonial is the historic heart of Santo Domingo. This square mile of cobbled streets and shady squares contains the oldest colonial buildings in the Western Hemisphere, including the cathedral. To walk along the Calle de las Damas is to retrace the steps of the first Spanish conquistadors, who used Santo Domingo as a base for the conquest of Latin America. Yet, this district is no museum piece. It's dotted with shops, restaurants, and cafés, many housed in colonial-era buildings. It is also a real neighborhood, where families sit outside their homes enjoying the cool of the evening.

Straw hats for sale at Parque Colón

🍴 The bustling Café El Conde, on the corner of Parque Colón, may not be the most luxurious establishment in town, but is ideal for a cold drink, snack or simple meal.

👕 Shorts and swimwear are not suitable for the city center, especially in churches and the Pantheon. Even poor Dominicans dress smartly, and they expect the same from visitors.

• Map N3
• Torre del Homenaje: Fortaleza Ozama; Open 9am–6pm daily; Adm $0.50
• The National Pantheon: Open 9am–6pm Mon–Sat; Free
• Alcázar de Colón: Open 9am–12pm, 2:30–5:30pm Tue–Sat; Adm $1
• Casa del Cordón: Open 9am–5pm Mon–Fri; Courtyard only; Free

Top 10 Sights
1. The Cathedral
2. Torre del Homenaje
3. Parque Colón
4. Calle de las Damas
5. The National Pantheon
6. Hostal Nicolás de Ovando
7. Las Atarazanas
8. Alcázar de Colón
9. Las Casas Reales
10. Casa del Cordón

The Cathedral
1 This exuberant mix of Gothic and Classical influences *(above)* dates back to 1540. It has survived earthquakes and pirate attacks, and was reputedly the resting place of Christopher Columbus. Its cool, dark interior contains magnificent monuments.

Torre del Homenaje
2 Built as a watchtower in 1503, Homage Tower *(right)* was used to sight approaching pirate raiders, but later served as a prison, even during Trujillo's dictatorship *(see p31).*

Parque Colón
3 Named after Columbus, the large open space is dominated by a grandiose statue of the explorer *(below).* The square's cafés are a good point for people-watching.

Calle de las Damas
4 A cobbled medieval thoroughfare, lined with museums and churches, the street contains some of the old city's most tastefully restored buildings.

5 The National Pantheon

Formerly a Jesuit monastery, this Neo-Classical building commemorates the country's independence heroes. A solemn atmosphere fills the large marble-lined interior, and a uniformed soldier stands guard over the eternal flame.

6 Hostal Nicolás de Ovando

This recently restored, hotel *(left)* is situated within the mansion of the colony's first governor and features the original balconies and Andalusian fountain. A great place to stay, with views of the Ozama River.

7 Las Atarazanas

A line of former warehouses, converted into shops and restaurants *(left)*. The 16th-century buildings also contain a small museum depicting maritime life in the colonial era including objects salvaged from the galleon *Concepción*.

8 Alcázar de Colón

The stately 2-story palace *(above)* built by Christopher Columbus's son, Diego, overlooks the river and the large Plaza España. This Moorish-influenced coral-stone mansion is Santo Domingo's most impressive colonial site.

9 Las Casas Reales

The Real Audiencia or Supreme Court once sat in this early 16th-century mansion, now a colonial museum. Look out for the *reloj del sol* (sundial), reputedly placed for judges to check the time.

10 Casa del Cordón

The House of the Rope *(right)* is said to be the first 2-story building in the Americas. Diego Columbus lived here while his palace was being built. Its façade is decorated by a chiseled sash-and-cord motif.

Drake's Destruction

Colonial Santo Domingo's heyday came to an abrupt end in 1586 when Sir Francis Drake's 20-strong fleet sailed upriver. Unopposed, the English indulged in a month-long orgy of looting and demolition, while the Protestant Sir Francis slung his hammock in the cathedral. Santo Domingo was ruined.

Santo Domingo: The Modern City

Beyond the Zona Colonial is a fast-moving metropolis of over two million people, where upmarket suburbs rub shoulders with bleak-looking shantytowns and where quiet parks and museums provide a respite from the capital's frenetic traffic. The city radiates inland from the river and coastline, moving from compact 19th-century barrios to the spread-out commercial districts of the modern uptown. Spanish and Caribbean influences, expressed in wrought-iron balconies and ornate gingerbread-style woodcarving, give way to functional concrete office blocks and suburbs.

Statue at Parque Mirador del Sur

Carriage at Malecón

🅐 On the corner of Calle El Conde and Calle Hostos, the Mercure Comercial hotel offers an air-conditioned bar and other facilities for the weary sightseer.

🕐 To request a free tour of the Palacio Nacional (Mon, Wed, & Fri), call 686 4771, ext 340. Permission may take a couple of days, and you are expected to look suitably dressed.

• Map E4
• Museo del Hombre Dominicano: Plaza de la Cultura; 688 9700; Open 10am–5pm Tue–Sun; Adm $1
• Palacio de Bellas Artes: Máximo Gómez & Independencia; 682 1325; Daily; Free
• Botanic Garden: Av Jardín Bótanico; 565 2860; Open 9am–6pm Tue–Sat; Adm $1
• Columbus Lighthouse: Open 9am–5pm daily; Adm $1

Top 10 Sights

1. The Malecón
2. Ciudad Nueva
3. Calle El Conde
4. Gazcue
5. Museo del Hombre Dominicano
6. Palacio Nacional
7. Palacio de Bellas Artes
8. Botanic Garden
9. Parque Mirador del Sur
10. Columbus Lighthouse (Faro a Colón)

1 The Malecón
Stretching several miles eastwards from the port, the Malecón also known as Avenida George Washington, is the city's breezy seafront boulevard, lined with high-rise hotels, restaurants, and bars *(above & p52)*.

2 Ciudad Nueva
Next to the Zona Colonial, this low-level neighborhood of narrow streets and plazas contains fine examples of 19th-century architecture and maintains the atmosphere of a traditional *barrio*.

3 Calle El Conde
The old town's main shopping street, the pedestrian-only thoroughfare is lined by stores and offices. The street is renowned for jewelers and shoe shops, and also for Dominican music and Haitian art *(see p52)*.

4 Gazcue
A leafy middle-class suburb dating from the 1930s, Gazcue's eccentric mix of buildings includes imitation chalets and half-timbered English-style architecture and a number of cafés and galleries.

5 Museo del Hombre Dominicano
Part of the Modernist 1970s Plaza de la Cultura complex, this collection of artifacts reveals the day-to-day life and rituals of the pre-Columbian Taino people *(right & p34)*.

9 Parque Mirador del Sur
A haven for joggers and walkers, this park is set in the affluent diplomatic district. The limestone cliffs on the northern edge contain a series of caves, one of which houses a restaurant and another the vast Guácara Taína nightclub.

10 Columbus Lighthouse (Faro a Colón)
Inaugurated in 1992 to celebrate the 500th anniversary of Columbus's arrival, this marble-clad monument *(above)* attracted fierce criticism as a tasteless waste of money. But the sheer scale of the cross-shaped edifice is impressive.

6 Palacio Nacional
Although the presidential palace *(above)* looks impregnable, you can visit this 1940s exercise in Neo-Classical pomp, with its mahogany furniture and hall of mirrors. It houses government departments.

7 Palacio de Bellas Artes
An austere Neo-Classical façade announces the aesthetic credentials of the city's Beaux-Arts headquarters. Decorating the stairway are murals by José Vela Zanetti.

8 Botanic Garden
In the northern suburb of Arroyo Hondo, the 450-acre garden *(above)* showcases the tropical wealth of the country's flora, featuring palms, a Japanese garden, and 300 varieties of orchid.

Gleave's Lighthouse
JL Gleave, a 24-year-old Manchester architecture student, beat over 450 rival designs in 1929 in an international competition to commemorate Columbus's landfall. Funds for construction failed to materialize, and work began in 1986, 20 years after Gleave died.

🔟 Constanza & "The Dominican Alps"

The cool uplands of the country's interior are a world apart, barely 50 miles (80 km) away from the tropical heat of Santo Domingo. Dominated by the towering Cordillera Central, the mountain range that forms the island's spine, the central region is a nature-lover's paradise of protected national parks, streams, and valleys. The gentle climate encourages crops such as strawberries, and at high altitudes frosts are not uncommon. The green meadows and pine forests are far from the usual image of the Caribbean, and Pico Duarte, the highest mountain in the Caribbean, dominates the scene.

Strawberries

⏱ The 30-mile (47-km) "road" between Jarabacoa and Constanza is generally considered too poor for most vehicles, but Iguana Mama *(see p127)* organizes a mountain bike journey along tracks that can reach 5,500 ft (1,676 m).

There are no gas stations on the lonely and sometimes impassable mountain roads around Jarabacoa and Constanza, so motorists should remember to fill up in town.

• Map C3
• *Rancho Baiguate: 574 6890; www.ranchobaiguate.com.do*
• *Salto de Jimenoa: Open 9am–7pm daily; Adm $0.50 • Salto de Baiguate: Open 9am–7pm daily; Free*
• *Parque Nacional Armando Bermúdez: Adm $5; Official guide compulsory*

Top 10 Sights

1. Jarabacoa
2. Balneario La Confluencia
3. Rancho Baiguate
4. Salto de Jimenoa
5. Salto de Baiguate
6. Constanza
7. Parque Nacional Armando Bermúdez
8. Reserva Científica Valle Nueva
9. Salto Agua Blanca
10. Pico Duarte

1 Jarabacoa

Once an isolated agricultural village, this small town has become a popular summer retreat and a base for walkers and sports enthusiasts. The Río Yaque del Norte runs close to town, tempting swimmers and rafters *(see p40)*.

2 Balneario La Confluencia

Jarabacoa's own natural swimming pool *(below)* was formed where the Yaque del Norte meets the Jimenoa just outside town. The water can be quite fast-moving when the rivers are high, and there is also a shady wooded park.

3 Rancho Baiguate

The best-organized adventure center in the area, this rustic complex *(above)* is set in attractive riverside grounds and offers a range of outings and activities as well as accommodation, a swimming pool, and a Dominican art gallery. Day visitors are welcome.

4 Salto de Jimenoa
This 131-ft (40-m) waterfall is reached via a hair-raisingly narrow suspension bridge. The cold water of the Río Yaque del Norte cascades noisily into an inviting pool, with lush vegetation surrounding the rocky canyon. At weekends a snack bar is open for visitors.

5 Salto de Baiguate
A scenic walk around a path cut into the edge of a ravine leads down to the valley floor where a torrent of water crashes into a swimming hole *(left)*, which is then reached on horseback.

6 Constanza
Set in a fertile valley ringed by mountains, the larger town of Constanza is an excellent starting point for hikes. The heart of the region's agricultural economy, it has a busy farmer's market *(left)*.

7 Parque Nacional Armando Bermúdez
The 289 sq-mile (750 sq-km) reserve *(above)* in the Cordillera Central is home to a stunning array of flora and fauna. The ranger station at La Ciénaga is the starting point for organized treks.

8 Reserva Científica Valle Nueva
The pot-holed and vertiginous mountain road from Constanza to San José de Ocoa traverses this remote protected zone, where impenetrable pine forests offer protection to countless species of birds.

9 Salto Agua Blanca
A long trek through rough mountainous terrain is amply rewarded by this spectacular 492-ft (150-m) waterfall, whose white water drops straight down into a pool. Ferns and other vegetation cling onto the sheer rock faces of the canyon.

10 Pico Duarte
Not officially climbed until 1944 and named after the father of independence, the peak is often shrouded in cloud. Visitors can also admire the mountain from a distance *(left & p40)*.

Japanese Dominicans
In the 1950s, the Dominican government imported 200 Japanese farming families to form an agricultural colony in Constanza and boost the town's economy. Some of their descendants still live in the area, and a Japanese social club thrives. However, the original Colonia Japonesa is now largely abandoned.

Visitors to Parque Nacional Armando Bermudez must register at the Park Office at La Ciénaga

🔟 Santiago

Santiago de los Caballeros (Santiago of the Gentlemen) *is the Dominican Republic's second city. From its founding in 1495 by the 30 Spanish noblemen* (caballeros), *this busy metropolis has considered itself wealthier and harder-working than the capital. Set in the fertile Cibao Valley, Santiago has historically been the hub of the country's agricultural riches, and its millionaire families largely owe their fortunes to the sugar and tobacco grown nearby. The city is calmer than Santo Domingo, but lively enough in Calle del Sol and around the landmark Monument to the Heroes.*

Calle del Sol

🔵 Santiago's most attractive cafés and restaurants are clustered around Calle del Sol. At weekends the surrounding area often becomes an open-air disco, with loud music.

🟢 A working tobacco factory off the Av 27 de Febrero, the Aurora Tabacalera, can be visited on week days. Here you can see top-class Dominican cigars being rolled and sample the local exports.

• Map C2
• *Palacio Consistorial: Open 9am–12pm, 2:30–6pm Tue–Fri; Free*
• *Museo del Tabaco: Open 9am–12pm, 2–5pm Tue–Fri; 9am–12pm Sat; Free*
• *Monumento a los Héroes de la Restauración: Open 9am–12pm, 2–5pm Mon–Sat; Free*
• *Bermúdez Rum Factory: Open 9am–12pm, 2–5pm Mon–Fri; Free; By appointment*

Top 10 Sights

1. Parque Duarte
2. Cathedral
3. Centro de Recreo
4. Calle del Sol
5. Palacio Consistorial
6. Mercado Modelo
7. Monumento a los Héroes de la Restauración
8. Museo del Tabaco
9. Gran Teatro del Cibao
10. Bermúdez Rum Factory

Parque Duarte
The heart of old Santiago, this pleasantly tree-filled space is a meeting-place for locals and a good spot for people-watching *(above)*. You can hire a horse-drawn carriage for a tour of the surrounding streets, or buy a merengue CD.

1839–1897

Cathedral
The pastel-shaded Catedral Santiago Apóstol *(left)* dates from the late 19th century, but its most eye-catching feature is its modern stained-glass windows. One of the country's dictatorial presidents and local boy, Ulíses Heureaux *(see p31)*, lies here in a marble tomb.

3 Centro de Recreo

Offering an unexpectedly exotic Moorish flavor, the Mudéjar-style private club testifies to the wealth of Santiago's 1890s sugar barons. An ornate façade of arches and pillars conceals an opulent interior of carved wooden ceilings and a grand ballroom.

4 Calle del Sol

The buzzing urban thoroughfare of Santiago, this street is lined with department stores, hotels, and sidewalk vendors. At night, shoppers and office workers give way to those in search of entertainment in its many bars and restaurants (see p55).

5 Palacio Consistorial

A proud civic structure, formerly the town hall, this fine example of Victorian-era Neo-Classical symmetry houses the city's museum and art gallery.

6 Mercado Modelo

A smaller equivalent of Santo Domingo's cavernous covered market (above), the green and white structure dates from the 1940s.

7 Monumento a los Héroes de la Restauración

The Monument to the Heroes (left) boasts a 230-ft (70-m) pillar topped by an allegorical figure of Victory. The marble edifice was commissioned by Trujillo and contains murals by Vela Zanetti, inspired by Mexican Diego Rivera.

8 Museo del Tabaco

Santiago's historic role as a cigar-producing center is presented in this former tobacco warehouse, with exhibition rooms. Visitors learn how the crop is grown and how cigars are rolled (left).

9 Gran Teatro del Cibao

Another monumental folly, the modern marble-clad theater is the 1980s legacy of President Balaguer (see p31), responsible also for Santo Domingo's Columbus Lighthouse. Its huge auditorium stages occasional opera.

10 Bermúdez Rum Factory

Very easily located in the northern suburb of Pueblo Nuevo, Bermúdez's processing and bottling plant (above) is happy to welcome visitors to inspect one of the country's premier brands in the making. A free tour is usually concluded with a free cocktail.

Liberation Struggles

Santiago played a crucial part in the struggle to oust the Spanish in 1863 after they had annexed the country. A force of over 6,000 guerrillas besieged the Spanish garrison until they surrendered, and a provisional government was set up in Santiago, but not before the city was almost destroyed by fire.

Centro de Recreo is a private club and usually closed to visitors, but members might show you around if you're properly dressed

Puerto Plata

The "Silver Port" lies between the glittering Atlantic Ocean and the imposing bulk of the Pico Isabel de Torres. Its roots go back to 1502, but it was during the 1970s that this once-sleepy provincial backwater was rejuvenated by the advent of mass tourism. The nearby resorts of Playa Dorada and Sosúa attract legions of visitors each year, but a tour of Puerto Plata's colorful center, complete with Victorian-era architecture, galleries, and restaurants should not be missed. A tight grid of central streets dates to the brief tobacco boom in the 19th century. This is the best place to soak up the atmosphere of a bygone golden age.

Parque Central
3 A shaded oasis, *(above)* surrounded by whitewashed Victorian architecture, this is the heart of old Puerto Plata and a pleasant place to sit in a café or park bench. Most of the town's quaint gingerbread buildings are clustered around the park.

Artifacts at the Museum of Taino Art

🍴 Sam's Bar & Grill, at 34 Calle Ariza, offers an expatriate atmosphere and good food and is a good place for local information.

⚡ The cable car can be closed during bad weather and often involves a long wait during peak tourist seasons. Check with your hotel before setting out.

• Map C1
• San Felipe Fortress: Open 8am–4pm daily; Adm $1 • Museum of Taino Art: Open 9am–5pm Mon–Fri; Free
• Museo del Ambar: Open 9am–5pm Mon–Sat; Adm $1.50 • Brugal Rum Factory: Open 9am–12pm, 2–5pm Mon–Fri; Free • Cable Car: Open 9am–4pm Mon–Sat; Adm $3

Top 10 Sights
1. San Felipe Fortress
2. Malecón
3. Parque Central
4. La Glorieta
5. Museum of Taino Art
6. San Felipe Cathedral
7. Museo del Ambar
8. Brugal Rum Factory
9. Pico Isabel de Torres
10. Cable Car

San Felipe Fortress
1 A solid-looking bastion *(right)* intended to deter marauding pirates in the 16th century, this brick-built fort — the oldest in the New World — has been restored and contains cannon and other weaponry from the colonial period in a small museum. You can also climb up the towers and gun turrets.

Malecón
2 Dominated by a heroic statue of independence hero General Gregorio Luperón on horseback, the seaside Malecón, loved by walkers and roller-skaters, offers uninterrupted views of ocean and mountains. This is also the venue for the vibrant annual Merengue Festival *(see p51)*.

La Glorieta
4 This 1960s reconstruction of the original gazebo *(below)* provides the focal point of the square. The symmetrical 2-story white-and-green wooden bandstand was apparently constructed to a Belgian blueprint in 1872.

5 Museum of Taino Art

Part of a large complex of art and handicrafts called Plaza Arawak, this collection of pre-Columbian artifacts explores the mysterious religious beliefs of the island's indigenous people.

6 San Felipe Cathedral

Recently given a facelift after the September 2003 earthquake, the twin-towered Catedral San Felipe Apóstol *(above)* is a successful blend of traditional colonial and Art Deco influences.

Bahía de Puerto Plata

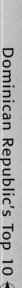

9 Pico Isabel de Torres

The 2,800-ft (850-m) peak offers a stunning bird's-eye view over the town and coastline. A smaller version of Rio's statue of Christ gazes protectively over the horizon, while a Botanic Garden makes for a pleasant stroll.

10 Cable Car

The *teleférico (above)* is the most spectacular way of reaching the summit: a smooth 20-minute ride up the Caribbean's only cable car system, over the wooded mountainside, with terrific views of Puerto Plata and the Atlantic Ocean.

7 Museo del Ambar

Housed in a German tobacco magnate's exquisite mansion, the museum *(above)* showcases the local amber industry, displaying finely-crafted jewelry as well as natural phenomena such as a million-year-old lizard trapped in a luminous block of the precious resin.

8 Brugal Rum Factory

A tour of the 1880s rum bottling plant reveals the extent of Dominicans' love affair with rum *(below)*. The production lines are an impressive sight, but the highlight is the gratis cocktail.

Tobacco Boom

A sudden upturn in world tobacco prices transformed sleepy Puerto Plata's fortunes in the 1870s, and the port became a magnet to merchants, including several German entrepreneurs, who traded in Cibao-grown tobacco. Their opulent dwellings, many now sadly dilapidated, are testimony to an age when the town was the Caribbean's richest.

🔟 La Isabela Bay

Set among some of the country's most rugged countryside and bordered by magnificent beaches, La Isabela breathes history as the site of the first permanent colonial settlement in the Americas. The bay protects a placid expanse of ocean, while a pristine white beach looks much as it must have done in 1493 when Christopher Columbus decided to establish a town on this spot, named in honor of the Spanish Queen. The excavated ruins of La Isabela give a powerful impression of that decisive moment, but it is the situation as much as the archeological display that makes this place special. An adventurous trek through remote terrain is rewarded by an unforgettable insight into how the course of history was changed.

Parque Nacional Histórico La Isabela

🌀 "Official" guides from the national park office are meant to accompany visitors and expect a tip. English-speaking Celestino Torres has been recommended.

The roads around La Isabela are potholed and often occupied by large herds of goats. Driving after dark is not a good idea.

• Map B1
• Parque Nacional Histórico La Isabela: Open 8am–5pm daily; Adm $3
• Museum: Open 9am–5:30pm Mon–Sat; Adm $2
• Templo de las Américas: Open 9am–5pm daily; Free
• Cayo Paraíso: www.cayoparaiso.com

Top 10 Sights

1. Parque Nacional Histórico La Isabela
2. The Settlement
3. Columbus's House
4. Cemetery
5. Museum
6. Playa Isabela
7. Templo de las Américas
8. Laguna Estero Hondo
9. Punta Rucia Beach
10. Cayo Paraíso

1 Parque Nacional Histórico La Isabela

A protected national park gradually excavated since the 1950s, the site of the original settlement sits on a promontory; an expanse of red sand dotted with acacia trees and criss-crossed by paths that lead visitors around the architectural remains *(below)*.

2 The Settlement

Small walls of roughly hewn limestone *(right)* trace the foundations of La Isabela's structures, including what are thought to be warehouses, a chapel, a rudimentary hospital, and a watchtower.

3 Columbus's House

On a slight bluff overlooking the site is the shell of the residence belonging to Columbus. Covered with a thatched awning, the ruin *(above)* shows that he lived in a modest dwelling made of packed earth and stone.

4 Cemetery
The New World's first Christian cemetery *(above)* occupies a scenic waterside position, decorated by the later addition of white crosses. Both Spaniards and Tainos were buried here, and in one grave a Christian skeleton was exhumed.

6 Playa Isabela
The beach, where the slow-moving Bajabonico River meets the sea, is an unspoilt stretch of sand, where tiny fishing boats bob offshore. Amenities are few, so come prepared *(right & p44)*.

7 Templo de las Américas
This colonial-style church *(below)* is a blend of whitewashed stone and brick, built in 1990, in time to celebrate the 500th anniversary of Columbus's arrival. Pope John Paul II said Mass here in 1992.

9 Punta Rucia Beach
This is a long expanse of soft-white sand and limpid water, where small restaurants and shops provide cold drinks and freshly caught fish.

10 Cayo Paraiso
A tiny speck of sun-bleached circular sand-bank surrounded by coral reef and aquamarine sea, the cay can be visited on an organized tour by speedboat from Punta Rucia or the village of Castillo.

5 Museum
The park's museum contains a compact but well-maintained display of Taino artifacts *(below)*, including pottery and arrowheads. The exhibits' captions are Spanish-only, but these are visually interesting and include a model of Columbus's ship, the *Santa Maria*.

8 Laguna Estero Hondo
You can explore one of the region's best-preserved mangrove forests with a boat trip through this wild lagoon. Gnarled mangrove thickets are home to many birds, and you may be fortunate enough to catch sight of a rare manatee *(see p67)*.

Trujillo's Blunder
La Isabela's archeological potential was recognized by the Dominican dictator Trujillo, but when he ordered workmen to tidy up the site in 1952 they were rather too zealous and reportedly bulldozed much of the remains into the sea. Locals and souvenir-hunters have also been responsible for removing valuable artifacts.

🔟 Las Terrenas

A tiny ramshackle fishing village only 30 years ago, Las Terrenas has developed into one of the Dominican Republic's most sought-after tourist centers. An influx of expatriates from North America and Europe has brought a wide array of guesthouses and restaurants, tailored to the independent traveler. But development has not ruined this welcoming seaside community's relaxed atmosphere. Lying on the North Coast of the Samaná Peninsula, a lush strip of land pushing out into the Atlantic, the town is blessed by the proximity of some of the country's most beautiful beaches and by spectacular countryside around. Extensive groves of coconut trees fringe expanses of white sand which slope gently and invitingly into clear warm water.

Painted walls of a beachside restaurant

⚡ ATMs in the village are often empty, especially in peak tourist periods. Make sure you have enough cash before you arrive.

Although undeniably attractive, coconut trees are dangerous, and deaths are known to occur from falling nuts. Avoid sitting directly below.

- Map F2
- Tourist office: Carretera Las Terrenas, Open 9am–12pm, 2–5pm Mon–Fri
- Stellina Diving Center, Hotel Cacao Beach: 868 4165; www. stellinadiving.com
- Beachside Restaurants: Le Lagon, 240 6603; La Bodega, 865 6868
- El Portillo Beach Club: 240 6100

Top 10 Attractions

1. Playa Las Terrenas
2. Diving
3. Beachside Restaurants
4. Haitian Art
5. Shopping
6. Nightlife
7. Playa Bonita
8. Playa Cosón
9. El Portillo Beach Club
10. Salto de Limón

1 Playa Las Terrenas
Stretching a mile in either direction from the small town center, the attractive beach *(right)* is clean and safe with ample shade. Heading westwards, Playa Cacao, close to small hotels and bars, is slightly more developed than the others.

2 Diving
Relatively unspoilt coral reefs lie close to Las Terrenas. Divers *(above)* are attracted to nearby Playa Las Ballenas, where a group of small islands stand just offshore. There are many dive shops, such as Stellina Diving Center, and snorkel hire shops.

3 Beachside Restaurants
Spread along the beach either side of the main intersection are many top-rate but informal fish eateries *(below)*. Fish with coconut is recommended. Early evenings are atmospheric with technicolor sunsets over the water.

4 Haitian Art
Naïve Haitian art is widely available and is often mediocre and mass-produced. The Haitian Caraïbes Art Gallery (below) has a good and reasonably-priced selection of wooden sculptures and voodoo-influenced images.

5 Shopping
For a small town, Las Terrenas offers a surprising range of shopping opportunities, from the small modern mall to outlets along the main street. Bargains can be had by bartering with stall-holders, especially near the beaches.

9 El Portillo Beach Club
One of the largest all-inclusive resorts (above), complete with its own airport, this complex offers various sporting and entertainment options. Day visitors can admire its beautiful beach from the bar.

10 Salto de Limón
A 130-ft (40-m) cascade of white water (above) ends up in a delightfully clear pool, reached by a one-hour horseback ride from El Limón village. The trek to this remote waterfall is through beautiful and fertile countryside.

7 Playa Bonita
The immaculate "Beautiful Beach" is fringed by coconut trees, in which guesthouses are hidden. Less crowded than Las Terrenas, and ideal for kids (left & p44).

8 Playa Cosón
This isolated curve of powdery white sand, limpid water, and palm groves looks every bit the idyllic image of the tourist brochures. A couple of fishermen's shacks sell cold drinks and grilled fish to this beach's few visitors.

6 Nightlife
Las Terrenas is rightly celebrated for its busy but laid-back after-dark ambience, particularly at weekends when locals and tourists mingle at an open-air street fair or visit its many bars.

A Growing Resort
The transformation of Las Terrenas from a remote fishing community to a thriving tourism center was fueled by Canadians, Swiss, and Germans, who fell in love with the place in the 1980s and invested in real estate and accommodation. The village's isolation was ended for ever by the opening of a paved road from Sánchez.

🔟 Costa del Coco

The "Coconut Coast", with its reef-protected white beaches and placid waters is the country's up-and-coming tourist mecca, challenging the North Coast as the number one resort area. Some 40 miles (64 km) of uninterrupted beach sweeps up the southeastern tip of the country, the endless vistas of sea, sand, and coconut trees broken only by clusters of low-level hotels and villas. Since the 1980s a bonanza of construction has seen huge self-contained tourist cities rise up along the waters' edge, their varied attractions and facilities cut off from the rest of the world. It is possible, should you wish, to escape the luxury of the hotel enclave and to explore the dramatic beaches – some calm, others wild – that stretch as far as the eye can see.

Relaxing by the beach

🪸 Despite successful initiatives to improve food hygiene standards, mass-produced hotel buffets can be risky. Whenever possible, eat only freshly prepared meat and fish.

Check the quality of the glass-bottom boat before paying for a trip, as there have been complaints in some cases that the "glass" is hard-to-see-through plastic.

• Map H4
• Manatí Park: Open 9am–6pm daily; 221 9444; Adm; www.manatipark.com

Top 10 Sights

1. Playa Punta Cana
2. Cabo Engaño
3. Bávaro Beach Hotels
4. Manatí Park
5. Beach Markets
6. Water Sports
7. Corticeto Beach
8. Horse Riding
9. Playa Macao
10. Boca de Maimón

1 Playa Punta Cana

Backed by the landscaped grounds of two massive resorts, this long strip of perfect sand leads into warm turquoise water *(right)*. Coconut trees provide much-needed shade, and only guests are allowed to use the resorts' facilities.

2 Cabo Engaño

The headland separating the two main tourist towns is a paradise for surfers as high winds whistle around the cape. A lighthouse marks the country's easternmost point, where winds and strong tides make swimming very risky.

3 Bávaro Beach Hotels

Bigger and more developed than Punta Cana, the resort is dominated by a single complex of modern hotels *(below)*, offering a plethora of restaurants, water sports, and other creature comforts. An 18-hole golf course is a green oasis within the sun-baked sand.

4 Manatí Park

This controversial natural theme park offers fascinating insights into the country's flora and fauna, as well as allowing visitors to swim with tame dolphins in a large pool or to watch performing horses do entertaining tricks *(see p37)*.

6 Water Sports

The Costa offers every conceivable beach activity, including diving, catamarans, and snorkeling in the limpid waters *(above)*. The calm conditions make for excellent visibility, and glass-bottom boats reveal an underwater world of coral and fish life.

9 Playa Macao

A primitive dirt road leads northwards from the all-inclusives, leaving behind the manicured sand and entering a different landscape of wild beaches, crashing surf, and tiny fishing villages. Swimming is not advised, except at the more protected cove at Macao *(below & p44)*.

10 Boca de Maimón

One of the remotest of the country's beaches, this empty wilderness of undeveloped beach and mangroves is divided by a river mouth and surrounded by marshes and lagoons, home to sea turtles. Local fishermen outnumber tourists in this isolated spot.

5 Beach Markets

Good bargains can be had at one of the several beach markets at Cabeza de Toro or Bávaro, where locals sell rum, handicrafts, and Haitian art.

7 Cortecito Beach

One of the few stretches of sand not claimed by the all-inclusive giants, Cortecito has a more authentically Dominican feel, with small restaurants, bars, and a cluster of souvenir stalls. The sand is just as fine as around the big hotels.

8 Horseback Riding

The empty expanses of beach on the Costa del Coco make an ideal place for beginners or experienced riders to hire a horse *(left)*.

Millionaire Paradise

Punta Cana and Bávaro cater to the masses, but the Costa del Coco has a more exclusive and hard-to-locate luxury resort, Los Corales. The multimillionaire Dominican-born fashion designer, Oscar de la Renta, and his friend Julio Iglesias own opulent properties here.

For more information on horseback riding See p42

23

🔟 La Romana

"King Sugar" still reigns in the southern port city of La Romana, a place dedicated to cutting, milling, and exporting sugar since 1917. The huge sugar mill, though damaged by 1998's Hurricane Georges, still dominates the town, and you are likely to see cane-filled trains trundling through the surrounding countryside. Tourism rather than sugar is now the town's main lifeblood, and its pride and joy is the nearby Casa de Campo resort. This tropical playground of beach, sports facilities, and exquisite gardens offers the most sophisticated choice of activities.

Teeth of the Dog golf course

☉ Casa de Campo is theoretically guests-only, but cruise ship passengers may book horseback riding or golf sessions whilst onboard.

Prices at restaurants in Altos de Chavón are considerably higher than in La Romana itself, although many believe the views are worth paying for.

• Map G4
• Casa de Campo: PO Box 140, La Romana; 523-3333; www. casadcampo.cc
• Teeth of the Dog: Open 8am–5pm daily; 523 3333; Adm $75–$150; Caddies & equipment hire extra
• Altos de Chavón: Daily; Free
• The Amphitheater: Daily; Free

Top 10 Sights

1. Parque Central
2. Casa de Campo
3. Mercado Municipal
4. Golf Course
5. Playa Minitas
6. Marina
7. Isla Catalina
8. Altos de Chavón
9. The Amphitheater
10. Río Chavón

Dominican Plaza, Altos de Chavón

1 Parque Central
The large and attractive square has been renovated since the hurricane and is bordered by the pretty Santa Rosa de Lima church *(above)*. This is the place for meeting the locals and visitors can also watch the early evening streetlife.

2 Casa de Campo
One of the world's premier resorts, this 700-acre expanse of beautifully tended gardens and tasteful villas is a world away from workaday La Romana *(see p72)*. Its sports facilities are second to none, and its undeniable prestige is reflected in its prices.

Dominican Plaza, Altos de Chavó

3 Mercado Municipal
This bustling market *(below)* is crammed with agricultural produce as well as handicrafts and other souvenirs of interest for visitors. The *botánicas* do not sell plants, but religious and magic items, often related to local beliefs and superstitions.

Golf Course
4 The internationally famous "Teeth of the Dog" course, with 8 holes right next to the Caribbean, is one of the region's most difficult. Day visitors are allowed to inspect *(left & p38)*.

Playa Minitas
5 A tiny and secluded strip of perfect sand sheltering behind a coral reef, this beach is reserved for guests of the Casa de Campo, although visitors are normally accepted.

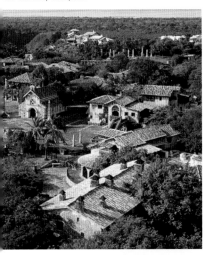

Marina
6 This modern water-side complex is intended for the well-heeled yachting enthusiasts who use the marina's mooring facilities. The crescent-shaped plaza *(right)* facing the yachts contains several up-market cafés, restaurants, and boutiques.

Isla Catalina
7 This tiny uninhabited island draws large crowds of excursionists from the Marina to a fine white beach, where Casa de Campo has set up tourist facilities. The diving off the North Coast is best.

Altos de Chavón
8 A bizarre replica of a Tuscan hillside village, the cluster of stone houses and plazas is both an arts center and a major tourist magnet. The imitation has attracted criticism, but many love the village's old-world air.

The Amphitheater
9 Altos de Chavón's most eye-catching feature is its 5,000-seat open-air amphitheater *(above)*, a vast limestone concert bowl inaugurated by Frank Sinatra in 1982. With Greek columns and spectacular views all around, it provides an impressive backdrop for big-name performances.

Río Chavón
10 Below Altos de Chavón, the river *(above)* moves slowly through a densely wooded gorge, where palm trees are reflected in the water. New Orleans-style paddle-boats ply this dark, enigmatic, and mysterious waterway.

Birthday Gift
The grandiose mock-Italian folly of Altos de Chavón was reputedly built by the president of Gulf & Western, Charles Bluhdorn, as a birthday gift to his daughter in 1976. Dominique Bluhdorn remains associated with the village as a leading light of the Altos de Chavón Cultural Center Foundation, more than 25 years later.

🔟 Lago Enriquillo

This vast inland stretch of salt water is more like a mini-sea than a lake. Glinting in an arid plain beneath rugged mountains, it marks the lowest geographical point in the entire Caribbean and is said to cover about the same area as Manhattan. Home to thousands of birds, iguanas, and American crocodiles, it is a protected National Park. Yet, the lake, its main island, and surrounding villages are easy to visit, offering a very different landscape from other parts of the island. Hot, dry, and sparsely inhabited, this border country stands in fascinating contrast to the developed coastal areas.

Shop at La Descubierta

🌀 There is a flat fee payable for the boat ride, irrespective of numbers, so it may be worth waiting for other visitors to share the cost (approximately $60).

It is impossible to cross the border in a rental car, and most crossings involve extensive bureaucratic obstacles and bribes, even for a few hours. It is much easier to fly.

• Map A4
• Boat Trips: Open 7:30am–1pm daily; Fare approx RD$1000

Top 10 Sights

1. Lago Enriquillo
2. Boat Trips
3. Isla Cabritos
4. Bird-watching
5. Crocodiles & Iguanas
6. Las Caritas
7. La Descubierta
8. Las Barias Balneario
9. Jimaní
10. Border Market

Boat Trips
2 Boats set off from the National Park Office to Isla Cabritos, and to ferry visitors to the crocodiles, which prefer the fresh water inlets on the northern shore. Boatmen will try to pass as close as possible to the sleepy beasts.

Isla Cabritos
3 A sandy spit of land with dry shrub and coral-strewn beaches, the Goat Island *(above)* provides perfect sanctuary to an iguana colony and some 500 crocodiles. A walk through the parched island reveals flowering cacti and scuttling lizards.

Bird-watching
4 This remote site is a haven for over 60 species of birds, many of which can be observed from the road or the water itself. The most identifiable are the flamingos *(left)*, which gather in huge numbers at dawn and dusk.

Lago Enriquillo
1 Girdled by a circular road, the huge lake stands under the intense sun. Dead tree trunks emerging from the water's edge testify to its saltiness and give it an eerie atmosphere, emphasized by the silence around *(above & p110)*.

Las Caritas is a wild, isolated cave, with no fixed times or admission charges

5 Crocodiles & Iguanas

Crocodiles can be secretive, especially when the heat rises and they take to the water, but the ricord and iguanas are not shy, approaching visitors in the hope of a snack. Feeding these large reptiles is discouraged.

9 Jimaní

The spread-out town of Jimaní marks one of the official border crossings into Haiti, although the frontier line is actually 3 miles (5 km) away down a very hot road. You are likely to see brightly painted Haitian buses *(above)*, known locally as *tap-taps*.

10 Border Market

The dusty no-man's land between the two countries is the scene of a semi-permanent outdoor market, in which Haitian traders sell mostly counterfeit clothing and watches. Haiti's celebrated Barbancourt rum *(right)* is worth buying.

6 Las Caritas

Easily found off the side of the road near the village of Postrer Río, an open cave reveals traces of early indigenous culture and religious ritual in the form of small faces *(caritas)* carved into the coral rock.

7 La Descubierta

A small and sleepy outpost of single-story houses, some brightly painted, the village stands in the middle of the hot plain. It has a shaded central square, a couple of short walking paths, and several cheap bars and restaurants.

8 Las Barias Balneario

A strange feature of La Descubierta is its cold natural pool of slightly sulfurous water *(above)*. Popular with local families, this *balneario*, with food and drink available nearby, also welcomes visitors.

Inland Sea

Lago Enriquillo is believed to have been linked to the bay of Port-au-Prince and the sea until tectonic shifts in the earth's surface about one million years ago closed this access and turned it into a lake. This explains both the saltiness and the presence of seashells and coral fragments.

There are no recommended restaurants in La Descubierta, but a number of stalls sell street food around the sulfur spring

Left **Columbus's House, La Isabela Bay** Right **Sir Francis Drake greeting a local chief**

🔟 Moments in History

1 c. 500 BC: Taino Culture
The Taino people arrive on the island they call Quisqueya after a centuries-long canoe-borne migration up the Caribbean archipelago from the Orinoco Delta in South America. A peaceful village-based society of fishermen and farmers, they worship gods of nature and the afterlife.

2 1492: Columbus Arrives
The Genoese explorer sets foot on Quisqueya, which he believes to be near China, and renames it Hispaniola. The discovery heralds the advent of Spanish colonialism as well as the rapid extermination of the Tainos. The city of Santo Domingo is founded in 1498.

3 1586: Francis Drake Sacks Santo Domingo
The golden age of the Spanish colony ends when the English privateer loots and vandalizes his way through its main town. By now, English, French, and Dutch pirates are a constant threat to Hispaniola and other Spanish colonies (see p9).

4 1697: Treaty of Ryswick
After many years of growing French presence in the west of the island, an agreement divides Hispaniola between French Saint Domingue and Spanish Santo Domingo. The French create a huge prosperous colony, based on slavery and sugar, while the underpopulated Spanish side languishes, dominated by large ranches and the Church.

5 1804: Haitian Independence
Following 13 years of revolution and civil war, an army of former slaves drives out Napoleon's troops from Saint Domingue, declaring Haitian independence. The Spanish colony is invaded and reinvaded, but is returned to Spanish rule in 1809. Santo Domingo fears Haitian territorial ambitions, and invades in 1821.

6 1844: Independence
Led by Juan Pablo Duarte, a group of nationalists stage a revolt against the 23-year-old Haitian occupation, declaring a separate, independent Dominican Republic. The Haitians are driven out after wealthy Dominican landowners recruit a peasant army. Duarte is quickly sidelined as regional *caudillos* (strongmen) struggle for political control.

7 1915–25: US Occupation
The Marines land in Santo Domingo to impose peace and "restore order" in a country wracked by infighting. The US presence brings foreign

Columbus's statue, Parque Colón

Previous pages **Exterior of Catedral Santa María de la Encarnación, Santo Domingo**

Trujillo's casket, Santo Domingo

investment in the sugar industry and throws peasants off their land. The occupation also creates a National Police Force, from which emerges Rafael Leonidas Trujillo, "the Benefactor".

8 1961: Assassination of Trujillo

Thirty years of brutal dictatorship come to an end when Trujillo is gunned down on Santo Domingo's Malecón. Trujillo had become enormously rich and all-powerful, imprisoning, exiling, and murdering his opponents. He even had the capital renamed Ciudad Trujillo in his honor. His death signals a gradual move towards democracy.

9 1970s: Arrival of Tourism

The first steps in creating a tourism industry take place with the building of hotels on the North Coast. Over the next three decades the country shrugs off its reliance on sugar and becomes a major player in Caribbean tourism, with resorts, airports, and cruise ships.

10 1996: First Fair Elections

A sorry record of voting fraud ends with the country's first free and fair elections. After 30 years of dominating politics, Trujillo's former puppet president, Joaquín Balaguer, is forced to retire at the age of 89, allowing Leonel Fernández to win.

Top 10 Heroes & Villains

1 Christopher Columbus (1451–1506)
Visionary explorer or deluded gold hunter? Opinions remain mixed on the man who started the Spanish colony.

2 Bartolomé de Las Casas (1474–1566)
Courageous priest who protested against the Spanish extermination of the Tainos to the King of Spain.

3 Enriquillo (1498–1535)
Leader of the last Taino revolt against the Spanish.

4 Sir Francis Drake (1540–1596)
Hated in the Spanish world as a Protestant bigot.

5 Jean-Pierre Boyer (1776–1850)
Power-hungry Haitian president who ordered the 1821 invasion, abolishing slavery but imposing a military rule.

6 Juan Pablo Duarte (1813–1873)
The revered father of the Dominican nation, a patriot who freed his country.

7 Ulíses Heureaux (1845–1899)
Dictator (1882–1899), who tried to sell the Germans a naval station in Samaná.

8 Trujillo (1891–1961)
The nastiest dictator of them all ordered the massacre of 15,000 Haitians in 1937.

9 María Montez (1912–1951)
Glamorous Barahona-born actress, who made it big in Hollywood in the 1940s.

10 Joaquín Balaguer (1906–2002)
A politician who didn't like losing, won six dubious elections from 1966 to 1994.

Left **Taino petroglyphs, Las Caritas** Center & Right **Exhibits from Museo Prehispánico**

Taino Indian Sites

1 El Pomier Caves
Officially a Reserva Antropológica, this network of bat-infested caves north of San Cristóbal contains the largest display of Taino wall paintings and rock drawings in the Caribbean. You can see mysterious spiritual symbols and scenes of day-to-day pre-Columbian life depicted here. ◎ *Map D4 • Open 9am–5pm daily • Adm*

2 Las Caritas
The "little faces" chiseled into the coral rock of the cave overlooking Lago Enriquillo have a range of expressions. Some represent Tanios praying. Local legend has it that the renegade Taino leader Enriquillo *(see p31)* hid in this cave while on the run from the Spanish. ◎ *Map A4*

Taino cave, Las Caritas

3 Peñon Gordo, Bayahibe
Part of the Parque Nacional del Este *(see p41)*, this cave system has some of the country's best-preserved Taino images on rock panels. A guardian figure, with large head and raised arms, watches over the low entrance of the first cave. ◎ *Map G5*

4 Cueva José Maria
Farther into Parque Nacional del Este and accessible only in the company of a park ranger, this cave holds 1,200 Taino pictographs referring not only to religious beliefs but also to the coming of the Spanish. Black charcoal drawings on white limestone walls clearly show a bearded Spanish face and sailing vessel. ◎ *Map G4*

5 Museo Prehispánico
This museum holds specimens of delicately carved jewelry and decorated pottery. The powerful spiritual dimension of Taino society is vividly brought to life by the clay *zemis*, depicting various gods, and by a ceremonial stool, apparently used in rituals by a village chieftain or *cacique*. ◎ *Map K1 • 179 San Martín & Lope de Vega, Santo Domingo • Open 9am–5pm Mon–Fri*

6 Cueva de las Maravillas
This complex of grottoes and labyrinths is a fascinating exhibition not only of Taino art forms but also stalactites, stalagmites, and other geological curiosities. The 472 pictographs and 19 petroglyphs depict human figures and various animals associated with death rituals. ◎ *Map F4 • Open 9am–5pm daily • Adm*

7 Los Indios de Chacuey
An indigenous (and much smaller) version of Stonehenge, in England, a circle of rocks

Taino village, La Isabela

surrounds a stone slab in the middle of a huge open space. Nearby, religious petroglyphs suggest that this was an important ceremonial center. ⊗ *Map A2*

8 La Isabela
The museum at the Parque Nacional Histórico La Isabela *(see p18)* highlights the everyday life in a Taino village. Outside are examples of an indigenous *bohío* or thatched dwelling, and gardens containing staple crops grown by Taino communities.

9 Parque Nacional Los Haitises
Inhospitable mangrove swamps and rocky terrain mean that the Taino sites can only be accessed through an organized boat trip. Caves within the park have extensive drawings, including scenes of hunting, birds, whales, and various faces.⊗ *Map E3*

10 Parque Submarino La Caleta
Best known for its diving among offshore wrecks, this park also contains an excavated Taino cemetery, discovered on the beach in the 1970s. A display of skeletons reveals that indigenous communities preferred to bury their dead in a crouched fetal position, in anticipation, apparently, of being reborn. ⊗ *Map E4*
• *Open 9am–6pm daily* • *Adm*

Top 10 Taino Legacies

1 Barbecue
The Tainos liked to cook their meat and fish over *barbacoas*, outdoor charcoal-fueled grills.

2 Bohío
A rectangular house of wooden walls and thatched roof, widely seen in rural areas and villages.

3 Canoe
One of many Taino words *(canoa)* and inventions still in use today.

4 Cassava
A mainstay of the pre-Columbian diet, this root is poisonous unless properly prepared into flour.

5 Hammock
The Taino *hamaca* was the favored sleeping arrangement, raising its occupants above rats and other pests.

6 Hurricane
Huracán was an awe-inspiring god, symbolizing the terrifying power and violence of the natural world.

7 Petroglyphs
The carvings of human faces, animals, and abstract forms scratched onto rock, often in caves.

8 Pictographs
Drawings, usually made with charcoal against a pale rockface, showing everyday and spiritual imagery.

9 Tobacco
The Taino revenge on the Western world: the addictive and dangerous habit of smoking *tabaco*.

10 Zemis
Idols or fetishes representing the many spirits, ancestral and natural, which the Tainos devoutly and religiously worshipped.

Dominican Republic's Top 10

Left & Right **Exhibits from Museo del Hombre Dominicano**

Top 10 Museums

1 Museo del Hombre Dominicano

Perhaps the country's best museum, its collection of pre-Columbian artifacts reveals the intricacy of indigenous sculpture in the shape of jewelry and religious figurines or *zemis*. Another display charts the impact of African slavery on culture with an eye-opening exhibition of carnival costumes and a model of a voodoo altar *(see p11)*. ⊗ Map L3 • Adm

2 Museo de las Casas Reales

The colonial period is highlighted in this museum, housed in the 16th-century governor's Supreme Court. Period paintings and furniture give a powerful taste of the luxurious lifestyle of the Spanish élite, while a collection of weapons shows how the Tanios were subjugated. ⊗ Map P5 • Calle Las Damas, Zona Colonial, Santo Domingo • Open 9am–5pm Tue–Sun • Adm

Museo del Hombre Dominicano

3 Museo Juan Pablo Duarte

Freedom fighter Pablo Duarte *(see p31)* is honored in this modest one-story house where he was born. The mementos mostly comprise documents and paintings, but the three elegant rooms also contain fine furniture and iconography relating to Duarte's underground independence organization,

La Trinitaria. ⊗ Map P5 • 308 Calle Isabel la Católica, Santo Domingo • Open 8am–2:30pm Mon–Fri • Adm

4 Museo de las Hermanas Mirabal

The small town of Salcedo is unexceptional, apart from its museum commemorating the lives and deaths of the three Mirabal sisters, courageous opponents of Trujillo, who were murdered on the orders of the dictator in 1960. The little family house contains a collection of photographs and every-day personal effects. ⊗ Map D2 • Salcedo-Tenares Road, Salcedo • 577 2704 • No fixed timings

5 Museo Nacional de Historia y Geografía

Part of the Modernist Plaza de la Cultura complex, the collection covers everything from Taino life to the US occupation, with an emphasis on struggles with Haiti. The most fascinating section deals with the excesses of the Trujillo period, including a bullet-riddled car, removed from the scene of his assassination. ⊗ Map L3 • Plaza de la Cultura, Santo Domingo • Open 10am–5pm Tue–Sun • Adm

6 Museo de la Familia Dominicana del Siglo XIX

The house in which this 19th-century collection of domestic items is kept is more interesting

Santo Domingo (see map, right), is home to the country's most impressive museums

than the museum itself.
The 1503 mansion contains the
only double Gothic window in
the Americas. This colonial gem
also exhibits the furniture and
personal effects of a well-to-do
Santo Domingo family. ✪ Map P6
• Casa de Tostado, Calle Arzobispo
Meriño, Santo Domingo • Open
9am–4pm Mon–Sat • Adm

7 Museo de Arte Moderno

The four-story modern art
gallery demonstrates the vitality
and range of contemporary
Dominican creativity. Permanent
exhibitions are interspersed
with temporary shows, revealing
a tension between bucolic
paintings of idealized rural life
and darker, more sinister
meditations on poverty and the
country's violent past. ✪ Map L3
• Plaza de la Cultura, Santo Domingo
• Open 9am–5pm Tue–Sun • Adm

8 Museo Bellapart

This museum is a surprising
oasis of fine art within an
uptown car showroom. The
private collection here encompasses big names of modern
Dominican art such as Jaime
Colson, the master of rustic
realism, and the Spanish
anarchist exile, José Vela Zanetti,
whose impressionistic celebration of peasant life forms the
centerpiece of the
swanky gallery. ✪ Map
K2 • Corner Av John F
Kennedy & Lambert
Peguero, Santo Domingo
• 541 7721 • Open
10am–6pm Mon–Fri

9 Museo de la Comunidad Judía de Sosúa

The small exhibition
next door to Sosúa's
synagogue tells the

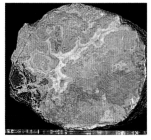

Larimar, Museo de Larimar

story of the country's Jewish
community, invited by Trujillo in
1940 to form an agricultural
colony. Photographs, letters, and
a sprinkling of 1940s artifacts
explain how they fled the Nazis,
settled in this North Coast town,
and started a dairy cooperative.
✪ Map D1 • Calle Dr Alejo Martínez,
Sosúa • Open 9am–1pm Mon–Fri

10 Museo de Larimar

One of the capital's newest
museums. An attractively
presented, multilingual exhibition
explains the process of mining
and shaping the semi-precious
blue stone into exquisite jewelry.
It's situated in a lovely colonial-
period house, where on the
ground floor you can buy fine
examples of larimar jewels.
✪ Map P6 • 54 Calle Isabel la Católica,
Santo Domingo • Open 8am–6pm
Mon–Sat, 8am–2pm Sun • Adm

For further information on Museo de Larimar log onto
www.larimarmuseum.com

Left **Horse-drawn carriages, Malecón** Center & Right **Columbus Aquapark**

Children's Activities

1 Acuario Nacional, Santo Domingo

Flanking the Caribbean Sea, the aquarium features a large plastic tunnel in which spectators are surrounded by water, sharks, rays, and conger eels. Colorful shoals of fish swarm around the tunnel, while exhibits explain different sorts of marine environments. The most popular family attraction, though, is an orphaned manatee *(see p71)*.
🄼 Map E4 • Av 28 de Febrero • 766 1709 • Open 9:30am–5:30pm Tue–Sun • Adm

Acuario Nacional

2 Agua Splash Caribe, Santo Domingo

This theme park has everything for swimmers and water-lovers, including 12 slides and pools of varying depth. There is ample shade, and refreshments are available. Weekends are extremely popular with local families. 🄼 Map P2 • Av España • 591 5927 • Open 10am–6pm Tue–Sun • Adm

3 Parque Zoológico Nacional, Santo Domingo

An expansive 400-acre park of tropical gardens and water features, the zoo is home to tigers as well as more local fauna such as flamingos and the elusive Dominican mammals, *hutías* and *solenodons*. Children will enjoy spotting creatures in sympathetically landscaped compounds as well as riding in the shuttle train. 🄼 Map K2 • Av de los Reyes Católicos • 562 3146 • Open 9am–6pm Tue–Sun • Adm

4 Horse-drawn Carriages

Small horse-drawn carts clip-clop up and down Santo Domingo's scenic Malecón as well as around the atmospheric Zona Colonial. Similarly relaxed and child-friendly sightseeing takes place in Santiago, where the focal point is the central Parque Duarte. Prices for a fixed time should be negotiated before you set off on that exciting ride.

5 Columbus Aquapark, Sosúa

A series of breathtaking rides down steep slides and through a cave are the highlights of this exceptionally popular water-based funfair. The large complex includes over 20 different rides, some more terrifying than others, and there is a gentle rafting excursion for those unwilling to try out the precipitous water-falls. 🄼 Map D1 • Carretera 5 • 571 2642 • Open 10am–6pm daily • Adm

6 Ocean World, Puerto Plata

This large new marine theme park offers interactive experiences such as swimming with bottlenose dolphins, exploring an imitation reef, feeding sea lions, and even getting close to sharks. There are many exhibits, a gift shop, and a restaurant too. Environmentalists are critical of the concept of keeping dolphins in captivity. ® Map C1 • Cofresí • 291 1000 • Open 9am–6pm daily • Adm

7 Manatí Park, Bávaro

Apart from the performing dolphins and horses, this park is a big hit with kids as it encourages them, under supervision, to hold non-poisonous snakes, as well as getting into a pool with dolphins. The emphasis is more on fun than education, and there are also several fast-food outlets (see p23). ® Map H4

8 Boca Chica Beach

Probably the safest and child-friendliest beach in the country, it lies inside a reef-protected cove with gently sloping sand and shallow water. You can wade out at low tide to a tiny offshore island, or build sandcastles or snorkel. ® Map F4

Horseback Riding, at El Limon

9 Horseback Riding

Almost every all-inclusive beach resort will either offer or be able to recommend horseback riding facilities. The small, normally patient Dominican horses are a good way to introduce kids to riding, especially on soft sand. More ambitious excursions in mountain terrain are available for experienced riders through specialist companies (see p42).

10 Baseball

Older children may enjoy the buzz of an evening baseball game, especially if familiar with the rules. The floodlit spectacle is usually accompanied by lots of music and razzmatazz as well as snacks galore. Children are welcome, though the game may end rather too late for younger ones (see p38).

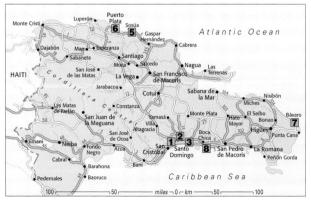

For more information on Ocean World log on to www.ocean-world.info

Left **Baseball at Parque Mirador del Sur** Right **Locals fishing**

🔟 Sports & Activities

1 Baseball
You can watch the local kids play, or have a go yourself at any local park, but to experience the fanaticism with which Dominicans follow baseball, you should visit one of the top gounds – Estadio Tetelo Vargas, San Pedro de Macorís *(see p72)* or La Romana *(see pp24–25)*.

2 Golf
The two top courses are integral parts of upmarket tourist resorts, but are open to non-residents. Designed by Pete Dye, Casa de Campo's challenging golf course in La Romana lies right next to the sea, as does the Robert Trent Jones course at Playa Dorada *(see p43)*. Other golf sites are the Punta Cana and Playa Grande *(see p89)*.

3 Tennis
You'll find tennis courts at all major hotels, and it's usually possible to hire rackets on site. The biggest complex is at Casa de Campo where professionals advise you on the game.

Golf course in Punta Cana Beach Resort

4 Basketball
Second to baseball in most Dominicans' affections, and growing all the time, this sport is played in every town and village by the locals, and there's nothing to stop visitors taking part. The main venue for serious games is Santo Domingo's Centro Olímpico, where the would-be professionals display their skills.

5 Cycling
Although cycling isn't safe in most towns and cities, the countryside is full of relatively quiet, if potholed, roads, and there is no shortage of off-road possibilities, especially in the Cordillera Central. Bikes can be hired from specialist tour operators *(see p127)*, who also lead organized excursions.

6 Fishing
Lake and river fishing are popular with locals, but angling-inclined visitors will want to have a go at deep-sea fishing, where sea bass and red snapper are favorites. For those who prefer a Hemingway-style contest, there is big-game fishing for marlin, setting out from Palmar de Ocóa and Cabeza de Toro.

7 Horse Racing
Dominicans like to bet, especially on cockfighting, but horses also have their fans, particularly at Santo Domingo's V Centenario racetrack. Here, gambling alternates with drinking.

The professional baseball season runs from November to February

8 Go-karting

With most adults happy to drive their cars at breakneck speed on the country's roads, this is normally reserved for children, although there's no reason why grown-ups can't roar around the corners. There's an excellent track on the Malecón at Santo Domingo and another good one inland from the Bávaro beach resort, Costa del Coco. Test your skills if gearing up to compete with your kids.
🐚 *Shell Kartodromo: Map M4; Malecón; 532 0552 • Tropical Racing: Map H4; Bávaro; 707 5164*

9 Bowling

Another United States import eagerly embraced by the Dominican youth, bowling has taken off as a popular family activity following the opening of a couple of state-of-the-art venues. The Sebelén Bowling Center in the capital is big and technically impressive, while Punta Cana has its own championship-standard alley. 🐚 *Sebelén Bowling Center: Map J3 • Plaza Bolero, Av Abraham Lincoln esquina Roberto Pastoriza, Santo Domingo • 920 0202*

Bowling

10 Polo

Legend has it that polo was introduced in 1954 by the Indian maharaja Jabar Singh, who was hired to teach the dictator Trujillo's sons. Its main home is now the exclusive Casa de Campo resort, where only the seriously rich can play, under the eye of the maharaja's sons. Visitors are also allowed to watch the matches during weekends. 🐚 *Casa de Campo: Map G4 • 523 3333 • www.casadecampo.cc*

Top 10 Baseball Players

1 Tetelo Vargas (1876–1981)
Revered in San Pedro de Macorís as a star outfielder and courageous opponent of dictator Rafael Trujillo.

2 'Ozzie' Virgil (b. 1932)
The first Dominican to make it big in the US Major League in the 1950s.

3 Felipe Alou (b. 1935)
This power hitter enjoyed a long career as a player and award-winning manager.

4 Juan Marichal (b. 1937)
Popularly known as the "Dominican Dandy" for his flamboyant style, Marichal was a record-breaking pitcher.

5 Ricardo Carty (b. 1939)
Carty was so impressive as a youngster that ten clubs tried to sign him up.

6 Tony Peña (b. 1957)
A four-time Golden Glover, he was an adept catcher and then a highly rated manager.

7 Sammy Sosa (b. 1968)
A household name, who rose from shoe shining to become a millionaire star and philanthropist.

8 Pedro Martínez (b. 1971)
Widely considered to be simply the best pitcher in the US Major League.

9 Vladimir Guerrero (b. 1976)
A massive and much-feared hitter, Guerrero combines a high level of speed, control, and accuracy.

10 Albert Pujols (b. 1980)
A member of the current generation of Dominican exports, and a rising superstar of powerful batting.

Left & Center **Waterfall & gorges near Jarabacoa** Right **View of Playa San Rafael**

🔟 Nature Trails

1 Pico Duarte
The biggest challenge of them all, the mountain can be reached from several trails, the most popular setting off from La Ciénega *(see p82)*. The round trip takes at least three days, and an official guide must accompany walkers. You'll pass through pine forests, meadows, and rocky terrain *(see p13)*. ◉ *Map C3*

2 Jarabacoa
The town provides the perfect base for walking or riding through the lush Dominican Alps *(see pp12–13)*, where waterfalls, clear rivers, and gorges are to be found among meadows and scented pine forests. There are many well-established trails in the area, varying from gentle strolls through farmland to day-long mountain treks. ◉ *Map C3*

3 Constanza
This idyllic, cool valley is the starting point for many recommended trails, which take you through pine forests and into flower-covered mountain meadows. Bird-watching is a big draw here, with Hispaniolan woodpeckers, parakeets, and hummingbirds in abundance. The trail to the Salto Agua Blanca is manageable and often spectacular *(see pp12–13)*.

4 Parque Nacional Monte Cristi
Most of this sprawling wilderness comprises desert and hard-to-reach mangrove swamps. But the large humpback mountain of El Morro is easily accessible from the park office, offering a great walk through a cutting onto the beach. This is the place to appreciate the Northwest's ecosystem *(see p95)*. ◉ *Map A1* • Daily • 472 4204 • Adm

5 Pico Isabel de Torres
If you don't want to take the cable car to the top of the mountain, you can always choose the four-hour hike up a steep

El Morro, Parque Nacional Monte Cristi

You may contact the park officers at the National Parks Office (DNP) at Av Independencia 539, Santo Domingo. Tel: 221 5340

Parque Nacional del Este

rainforest-clad slope. Guides are recommended, as it's easy to stray off the paths and get lost. The lush vegetation is home to parakeets and many other birds (see pp17 & 47). ⊗ Map C1

6 Punta Bonita
The walk from Las Terrenas (see pp20–21) to the gorgeous Playa Bonita (see p44) includes some of the country's prettiest beach scenery, with a shade-providing background of coconut groves. The headland of Punta Bonita is harder going over a stony hillside, but a path leads through a panorama of vegetation and boulders. ⊗ Map F2

7 Parque Nacional del Este
This large area of wilderness contains dry tropical forest and the Robinson Crusoe Island of Saona. An official guide must be hired, and a boat trip from Bayahibe is the best way to reach the otherwise inaccessible nature trails (see p73). ⊗ Map G5

8 Baní Dunes
The extensive dunes on the Las Salinas peninsula (see p109) are one of the country's best-kept secrets. An expanse of sandy hummocks, dotted with sea grape and marine grasses, rolls down to the glittering Caribbean. ⊗ Map D5

9 San Rafael
Inland from the deservedly popular beach and swimming hole, the river that fills the pool flows and falls down a hillside covered with boulders, ferns, and tropical trees. A hike up the riverside path passes a series of small waterfalls and leads to magnificent sea views. ⊗ Map B5

10 Parque Nacional Baoruco
Baoruco boasts the greatest variety of landscapes and flora, ranging from dust-dry, low-level hillsides to exuberantly tropical rainforests. A four-wheel-drive is essential to get to the profusion of wild orchids and swathes of pine forest. ⊗ Map A5

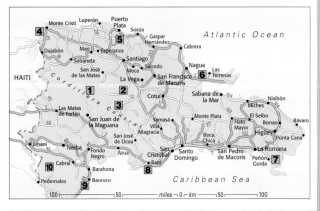

For further information on National Parks, log on to www.dominicanrepinfo.com/Parks-Reserves

Left **Playa Dorada** Center **Windsurfing at Bávaro Resort** Right **Starfish, Parque Nacional del Este**

Beach & Sea Activities

1 Swimming
There are good swimming options all around the country, but as a general rule the beaches on the South Caribbean coast have calmer waters than those on the Atlantic north. While some resort beaches have lifeguards, most public ones do not, and it is worth being cautious of strong currents.

2 Windsurfing
The placid waters of the South Coast are probably the best bet for novices, but Cabarete, with its powerful tides, is a magnet for true aficionados, drawing world-class competitors to the annual World Cup Windsurfing Competition in June. Equipment, of varying quality, can be hired from most seaside hotels. You may also get your training lessons at the Carib Bic Center. ✪ *Carib Bic Center: Map D1 • 571 0640 • www.caribwind.com*

3 Kitesurfing
Also centered around the surging surf beaches of the Cabarete area, this relatively new sport is growing in popularity because the use of a huge kite to produce momentum requires less wind than does a windsurfer's sail. With a following breeze, good kitesurfers can make huge leaps. Kitexcite specializes in this sport. ✪ *Kitexcite: Map D1 • 571 9509 • www.kitexcite.com*

4 Jetskiing
These high-speed mini power boats are a familiar sight, bouncing off the water at the established tourist resorts. Hire one and take a quick lesson in steering. Caution is required because accidents with swimmers and other, slower craft can all too easily occur.

5 Scuba Diving
Most dive companies are owned by Europeans or North Americans, who offer training as well as rental equipment. Diving around the country is incredibly varied, yielding up 16th-century shipwrecks, coral reefs, and marine life. Try the Tropical Dive Centre, Tropic Banana Hotel at Las Terrenas *(see pp20–21)* or Viva Diving, Bayahibe. ✪ *Tropical Dive Centre: Map F2; 481 0178 • Viva Diving: Map G4; 686 5658*

6 Horseback Riding
The beaches of the Costa del Coco *(see pp22–23)* are an ideal place for horseback riding against a scenic background of sea and coconut trees. Hotels and tour operators can easily make arrangements. ✪ *Sea Horse Ranch: Map D1 • near Sosúa • 571 3880*

Horse riding

7 Cavern Diving
The country's rugged limestone terrain is riddled with underwater caves and canyons

For more information on Sea Horse Ranch log on to www.sea-horse-ranch.com

which can be explored by experienced divers. You can swim through some tunnels, and examine the huge sponges and other sea creatures that live in the half-light of this submarine world. Caradonna can plan your diving tours. ◈ *Caradonna Caribbean Tours: 330 3322 • www.caradonna.com*

Catamaran Trips
8 A pleasure ride on a catamaran is a favorite and is on offer at every beach hotel. It normally involves a couple of hours at sea, followed by a stop at a cove where drinks and lunch are served. El Caballo can organize such trips. ◈ *El Caballo Tours: 240 6249 • www.elcaballotours.com*

Sail boats, Luperón

Sail Boats
9 Boats and catamarans are available at the main tourist resorts in the country. A good option is the small Hobie One cat (boats), to be found as part of all-inclusive packages at places such as Bávaro, Boca Chica *(see p71)*, Puerto Plata, Punta Cana, and Bayahibe.

Snorkeling
10 A snorkel and mask allows you to enter a multicolored underwater world of rocks, reefs, and teeming fish. The beaches around Las Terrenas are recommended as a good base for snorkeling.

Top 10 Activity Beaches

1 Cabarete
The best-known and sometimes busiest beach for all sorts of surfing. ◈ *Map D1*

2 Las Salinas
Another firm favorite with surfers, a white-sand beach set among saltpans and rolling dunes. ◈ *Map C5*

3 Playa Punta Cana
This long strip of soft sand offers plenty of scope for kayaking, sailing, and snorkeling. ◈ *Map H5*

4 Playa Bávaro
Another well-equipped stretch of beach, where independent dive operators compete with the all-inclusive amenities. ◈ *Map H4*

5 Playa Dorada
A beach of pristine sand, ideal for paragliding and building sandcastles. ◈ *Map C1*

6 El Portillo
Home of the Samaná Peninsula's biggest all-inclusive, this popular beach features every possible sporting activity. ◈ *Map F2*

7 Sosúa
A protected crescent cove in the town's center with an easily accessible reef that attracts snorkelers. ◈ *Map D1*

8 Playa Dominicus
Surrounded by all-inclusive resorts, this safe beach is great for windsurfing and kayaking. ◈ *Map G4*

9 Las Terrenas
Many activities are available, including swimming and snorkeling. ◈ *Map F2*

10 Boca Chica
Packed at weekends, the gently sloping beach is ideal for undemanding snorkeling and swimming. ◈ *Map F4*

Left **Playa Isabela** Right **Playa Rincón**

🔟 Quiet Beaches

1 Playa del Morro
A rocky track cuts through a gap in the landmark mountain of El Morro, leading to a deserted white-sand beach. The beach is walled in by sheet cliffs, but the water is calm and protected in this spectacular cove. Sunsets are superb. ◈ *Map A1*

2 Playa Isabela
Steeped in history, as the site of the first permanent European settlement in the Americas, this low-key stretch of sand backed by shade-giving vegetation attracts more fishermen than tourists. The freshwater Bajabonico River meets the sea at this spot, producing an interesting ecosystem that's worth exploring. ◈ *Map B1*

3 Playa Bonita
This is probably the nearest thing to the classic image of tropical paradise. White sand meets calm turquoise sea,

Boats, Playa Isabela

watched over by a stretch of coconut palms. Even the nearby hotels and guesthouses fail to intrude on the peaceful beach heaven *(see p21)*. ◈ *Map E2*

4 Playa Rincón
Lack of easy access due to a single connecting rough road, has kept this horseshoe cove free from obtrusive development. But there are plans afoot to site a new hotel complex here. The sand is pristinely white, the sea bluer than blue, and the coconut trees sway enticingly *(see p102)*. ◈ *Map F2*

5 Playa Limón
A beach for exploring rather than swimming. A long, wild, deserted 6-mile (10-km) stretch, where big breakers crash onto the palm-littered sand. As part of a protected National Park, the beach has escaped development and offers nature in the wild, including mangroves, coconut groves, and hungry mosquitoes. ◈ *Map G3*

6 Playa Macao
Only a few miles from the well-tended beaches of Bávaro and Punta Cana, this long, sweeping stretch of untamed coastline is as undeveloped as anywhere in the country. Pounding surf and a powerful undertow discourage most swimmers, but the bay at Punta Macao, with its sheltering headlands, is safer. ◈ *Map H3*

7 Playa Corbanito

The gray sand may not be the finest in the Dominican Republic, but the view over the Bahía de Ocoa towards the distant sierra is breathtaking. The bay's water is calm and inviting, and the beach itself, untroubled by tourists and home only to a few fishermen, is attractive and extremely relaxing. ✪ Map C5

8 Playa Baoruco

Harboring one of the many small and undeveloped beaches on the coastline south of Barahona *(see p110)*, Baoruco is more a fishing village than a tourist resort, although an all-inclusive hotel has recently opened nearby. The pretty beach has rather rough white sand, but the views into the wooded mountains are stunning. ✪ Map B5

Baoruco Beach Resort, Baoruco

Playa Cabo Rojo

9 Playa Cabo Rojo

Lying on the coastline of Parque Nacional Jaragua *(see p111)*, Red Cape is named for the rich red seams of bauxite that once fed a now-derelict processing plant. The wildness is certainly a draw for the penguins and other birds. ✪ Map A6

10 Playa Pedernales

As close as you can get to Haiti without crossing the border, this deserted beach overlooks a calm sea and offers great views of the Cabo Rojo headland to the south. Facilities here are minimal, but most evenings the beach comes to life when fishing boats return home to the village. ✪ Map A5

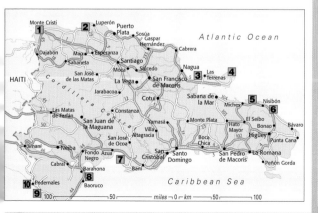

Left **Santo Cerro** Right **View from the San Felipe Fortress, Puerto Plata**

Top 10 Views

1 Torre del Homenaje, Santo Domingo

After a challenging climb up a spiral staircase, look out to the mouth of the Ozama River and across the water at the looming Columbus Lighthouse. Best of all is the panoramic view of the Zona Colonial, a grid of low-level whitewashed buildings nestling amid lush tropical trees. *Map P5 • Calle Las Damas • Open 9am–7pm Mon–Sat, 10am–3pm Sun • Adm*

2 Carretera 12

The winding but well-maintained road leading up from Bonao *(see p80)* to the Constanza Valley is one of the country's most fabulous. It meanders through pine forests and over rushing streams. As the temperature drops, there are superb views of the mountain range and the valley. *Map C3*

3 Santo Cerro

The site of a Spanish victory over the Tainos and a holy pilgrimage place, this mountain-top church is surrounded by a belvedere from where views extend for miles over the fertile Cibao Valley. The forested mountains and green valley floor might look European were it not for the palm trees *(see p81)*. *Map D2*

4 Pico Duarte

This peak offers excellent views, though only the toughest hikers can undertake the expedition to the top of the Caribbean's highest mountain. On a clear day, the Caribbean Sea can be seen to the south and huge Lago Enriquillo to the west *(see pp13 & 40)*.

5 Monumento a los Héroes, Santiago

Trujillo's monument is not to everyone's taste, but a climb to the top of the tower results in a wonderful view over the surprisingly large city and the surrounding countryside. The lift, alas, is out of use, but the exertion is well worth the effort *(see pp15 & 52)*. *Map C2*

View of Ozama River from Torre del Homanaje

6 San Felipe Fortress, Puerto Plata

Standing on the battlements of this ancient bastion situated on a promontory, behold the Atlantic, over the calm Puerto Plata Bay, or the majestic Pico Isabel de Torres (see p17). Late afternoons are spectacular, as the mountain changes color with the setting sun (see p16). ✎ Map C1

7 Pico Isabel de Torres, Puerto Plata

Watched over by a 54-ft (16-m) statue of Christ, the long Atlantic coastline stretches to the horizon. You can find hotel clusters and other modern developments lined along the white beaches. The town of Puerto Plata (see pp16-17) lies beneath, the cathedral clearly visible, and inland the mountains of the Cordillera Septentrional. ✎ Map C1

8 Naranjita

The serpentine road linking the beach resort of Las Terrenas (see pp20–21 & 102) to the town of Sánchez works its way over the spine of the peninsula, reaching 1,312 ft (400 m) near Naranjita village. From the roadside you can take in enormous

View of Río Chavón from Altos de Chavón

vistas of coconut trees, offshore islands, and the coastline ahead. ✎ Map F2 • Samaná Peninsula

9 Altos de Chavón

This mock Tuscan village stands on a bluff commanding wonderful views of the Chavón River, as it flows gently through a wooded ravine. Thick forest sweeps down to the water's edge, bordered by coconut trees (see p25). ✎ Map G4

10 Corbanito

A long, gray-sand beach backed by a few fishermen's huts and palm trees faces the Bahía de Ocoa, a calm inlet of glittering water ringed by mountains. The view across the bay is a marvelous mix of distant hillsides and sky, while the imposing Sierra El Número mountain rises behind. ✎ Map D5

Left & Center **Catedral Santa María de la Encarnación** Right **Catedral de Santiago Apóstol**

🗐 Places of Worship

1 Capilla de la Virgen del Rosario, Santo Domingo

Marooned on the industrial eastern side of the Ozama River, this tiny chapel is a reminder of the country's original capital. The existing church is a simple white-washed structure, with three brick portals, and dates from the 19th century, but the first wooden chapel was built in 1498.
◈ *Map P5 • Av Olegario Vargas • Open 10:30am–4pm daily*

2 Catedral Santa María de la Encarnación, Santo Domingo

The oldest cathedral in the Americas, this imposing building is a treasure trove of Gothic, Baroque, and Renaissance styles, with a mahogany altar, elaborate friezes and sculptures, and stained-glass windows. There are 14 separate chapels inside, one of which housed the remains of Columbus. ◈ *Map P5 • Parque Colón • Open 8am–4pm daily*

3 Santa Bárbara, Santo Domingo

The uncertain nature of colonial life is dramatically reflected by this asymmetrical church-cum-fort, dedicated to the patron saint of soldiers and explosives. The church was vandalized by Sir Francis Drake's pirates in 1586, and later damaged by a hurricane.
◈ *Map P4 • Calle Isabela la Católica • Open 8am–7pm daily*

4 Iglesia Parroquial, San Cristóbal

The massive mustard-colored parish church, with an imposing tree-lined plaza in front, was built in 1946 at huge public cost by the dictator Trujillo to honor his hometown. ◈ *Map D4 • Parque Duarte • Open 8am–5pm daily*

5 Catedral de Santiago Apóstol, Santiago

Look out for the fine carvings on the 1895 cathedral's mahogany doors, showing biblical scenes associated with St. James. Although it's often closed, the three-aisled interior is worth a visit for the marble tomb of Ulíses Heureaux *(see p31)*, and its modern windows by contemporary artist Rincón Mora. ◈ *Map C2 • Parque Duarte • Open 8am–5pm daily*

6 Catedral San Felipe, Puerto Plata

A symmetrical blend of old and new, the recently renovated cathedral dominates the historic center of town, with its two whitewashed, reinforced-concrete towers visible from afar *(see p17)*.
◈ *Map C1 • Calle Duarte • Open 9am–5pm daily*

7 Jewish Synagogue, Sosúa

A poignant reminder of the Jewish community that fled Nazi Germany to start a colony here, this

Detail on the door Catedral San Felipe

Iglesia San Pedro Apóstol

modest one-room synagogue, with its distinctive Star of David motifs, is housed in a simple but attractive wooden building. ◈ *Map D1 • Calle Martínez • By appointment*

8 La Churcha, Samaná
This red-roofed Non-Conformist church is made of prefabricated parts, sent from England by Methodists in 1823 to cater for English-speaking former slaves from North America who settled here under Haitian rule. ◈ *Map F2 • Santa Bárbara & Duarte • Open 9am–5pm daily*

9 Basílica de Nuestra Señora de la Altagracia, Higüey
The Republic's biggest church was designed in the 1950s to replace the smaller original as the site of the annual January 21 pilgrimage in honor of the Virgin of Altagracia, the nation's patron saint *(see p50)*. ◈ *Map G4 • La Altagracia • Open 9am–5pm daily*

10 Iglesia San Pedro Apóstol, San Pedro de Macorís
This landmark church, with its tall turreted bell-tower features a Romanesque doorway, Gothic-style gargoyles, and an imitation rose window. Built in 1911, it has long-standing associations with the English-speaking *cocolos*. ◈ *Map F4 • Av Independencia & Calle Charro • Open 9am–5pm daily*

Top 10 Religious Buildings in the Zona Colonial

1 Casa de los Jesuitas (1508)
The building, with a fine courtyard, housed a Jesuit-run school of rhetoric. ◈ *Map P5*

2 Monasterio de San Francisco (1508)
The ruins of the New World's first monastery are also used for concerts. ◈ *Map N5*

3 Hospital San Nicolás de Barí (1503)
The Americas' first hospital, now in ruins, was built in the shape of a cross. ◈ *Map N5*

4 Iglesia de la Altagracia (1922)
This Victorian church is famous for its miracle cures. ◈ *Map N5*

5 Iglesia Santa Clara (1552)
The first Franciscan nunnery in the Americas. ◈ *Map P6*

6 Convento de los Dominicos (1510)
This building became the first university in the Americas in 1538. ◈ *Map N6*

7 Iglesia Regina Angelorum (1537)
This forbidding structure's most impressive feature is its rich Baroque altar. ◈ *Map N6*

8 Iglesia San Lázaro (1650)
This church-hospital specialized in caring for lepers. ◈ *Map N5*

9 Iglesia del Carmen (1590)
Duarte's secret Trinitaria organization met here to plot the fight for independence. ◈ *Map N6*

10 Iglesia de Nuestra Señora de las Mercedes (1555)
The church has a distinctive mahogany pulpit. ◈ *Map N5*

Dominican Republic's Top 10

Cocolos *migrated here from the British Caribbean in the late 19th century*

Left **Carnival masks, La Vega** Right **Carnival parade on Independence Day**

🔟 Festivals & Holidays

1 New Year's Day

Dominicans welcome the New Year with an exuberant open-air concert on the riverside Avenida Francisco Alberto Caamaño Deñó, Santo Domingo, where some of the country's top bands perform. Other towns and villages hold smaller-scale but equally loud outdoor fiestas.

2 Three Kings' Day

The big present-giving day is a crucial part of the extended Christmas–New Year holiday season. In San Pedro de Macorís, some of the town's millionaire baseball stars traditionally hand out bats, balls, and gloves to kids. ◑ *Jan 6*

3 Virgen de Altagracia

The annual pilgrimage to the modern concrete basilica of Higüey brings thousands of Dominicans together in prayer to the nation's patron saint, followed by a long party. Services and vigils are held across the country, but the Higüey gathering is the most impressive expression of an African-influenced Catholic faith. ◑ *Jan 21*

4 Carnival

Every Dominican village, town, and city organizes some sort of event in the last week of February. La Vega *(see p81)* is famous for its devil-like Carnival masks, while the northern city of Monte Cristi *(see p95)* witnesses boisterous street battles between rival factions. ◑ *End Feb*

5 Independence Day

The Carnival period reaches an ear-splitting climax in Santo Domingo with a parade of costumes and bands along the Malecón. This also marks the anniversary of the country's independence from Haitian occupation. ◑ *Feb 27*

Devil costume, Carnival

6 Holy Week

As in all Latin countries, Semana Santa is the year's most important religious period, and all activity grinds to a halt as Dominicans go to church or parties or both. The Catholic celebrations are paralleled by African-influenced *vodu* (voodoo) ceremonies near the border and in the sugar plantations where Haitian migrants live. ◑ *Mid–April*

7 Merengue Festival

The latter part of the month witnesses a spectacular showcase of Dominican musical talent, as the seafront Malecón in Santo Domingo hosts a series of concerts by household names and newcomers alike. ◑ *July*

Restoration Day

8 The grandiose Monumento a los Héroes de la Restauración *(see p15)* is the scene of a huge party to commemorate the country's "second independence" from Spain in 1865 after a guerrilla struggle that started in Santiago *(see pp14 & 81)*. Another celebration, with plenty of music, takes place in Santo Domingo's beautiful Plaza España. ◈ *Aug 16*

Merengue Festival

9 In the third week in October, the northern port of Puerto Plata hosts a week-long celebration of merengue talent. Most of the action takes place on the long and normally rather rundown Malecón, but at this time of year the place comes to life, with bands performing and countless outdoor bars. ◈ *Oct*

All Souls

10 Both Catholics and followers of *vodu* celebrate the Day of the Dead, when, as elsewhere in Latin America and the Caribbean, families visit cemeteries to commune with the deceased, and take small offerings such as flowers and food. This ritual is taken most seriously in the areas near the Haitian border. ◈ *Nov 1*

All Souls celebrations: Day of the Dead

Top 10 Local Festivals

Azua (Mar 19)

1 A big patriotic celebration commemorating a historic Dominican victory over Haitian forces in 1844.

Puerto Plata (May 3)

2 The northern town noisily celebrates San Felipe, the votive day of its local saint.

Monte Cristi (May 30)

3 Fernando Rey festivities are in honor of the 16th-century Spanish monarch, turned into local patron saint.

San Juan de la Maguana (June 17–24)

4 San Juan Bautista, or Saint John the Baptist, is revered in this folkloric religious festival.

San Pedro de Macorís (June 29)

5 The city celebrates its patron saint, San Pedro Apóstol, with lots of music and dance.

Santiago (July 24–26)

6 Santiago Apostól, or Saint James the scourge of the Moors, is the object of great veneration.

Higüey (Aug 14)

7 The cowboy country lets its hair down with a rustic Festival of the Bulls.

Baní (Nov 21)

8 Images of Nuestra Señora de Regla, the town's adopted saint, are carried through the streets in celebration.

Boca Chica (Nov 30)

9 San Andrés or Saint Andrew has his lively *fiesta patronal* in the South Coast tourist town.

Samaná (Dec 4)

10 Santa Bárbara's day is the pretext for processions and partying in Santa Bárbara de Samaná *(see p101)*. The local popular music *bamboula* is played.

Left **Monumento a los Héroes** Center & Right **Tourists & locals at Boca Chica Beach**

⬛10 Places to Meet the Locals

1 Parque Central
Every Dominican town has its own central plaza, shaded by trees, supplied with benches, and often filled with locals. This is the place for people-watching, especially in the early evening, when most of them stroll around. Don't be afraid to smile and say what you can in Spanish.

2 The Malecón
Every evening, the capital's seafront boulevard attracts crowds in search of a cooling breeze. There are open-air bars and other seating areas, and you're bound to strike up a conversation sooner or later. Of course, there are some hustlers, but lots of friendly family groups fill the place, especially on Sundays *(see p10)*. ✎ *Map M4*

Haitian art for sale at the Malecón

3 Calle El Conde
This pedestrian-only shopping strip isn't the prettiest in town, but it's always full of life. Escape the heat and bustle outside by slipping into one of the bars or cafés and you'll meet plenty of visitors *(see p10)*. ✎ *Map N5*

4 Parque Mirador del Sur
A large and pleasant expanse of well-tended grass, trees, and tracks, the park is a magnet for joggers skateboarders, and dog walkers. Younger, health-conscious city dwellers congregate here along with families, especially in the morning and evening, when the through road is shut to cars *(see p11)*. ✎ *Map J4*

5 Monumento a los Héroes de la Restauración
Trujillo's folly is famous for its view, but the large open space around the monument is also a favorite among locals for meeting and having a good time. There are several friendly cafés in the vicinity, but the action gets going at weekends and public holidays *(see pp15 & 46)*.

6 Public Beaches
Although a few beaches are legally private, locals are often discouraged from using the sand near tourist complexes. So it makes a change to visit a public beach such as Boca Chica or Juan Dolio, where Dominican families enjoy themselves in a loud and uninhibited way.

7 Baseball Games
Watching a Dominican baseball game is as much a social as a sporting experience. The crowds are passionate but good-natured and the match is interspersed with a lot of chat,

drinking, and snacks. If you're interested in this sport, you'll make new friends *(see p38)*.

8 Carnival
Carnival is a countrywide affair in February, bringing out the most gregarious side of the Dominican character with days of merengue music and rum. Some of the traditional rituals can be rather boisterous and onlookers are likely to be squirted with water, but the emphasis is very much on fun *(see p50)*.

Carnival reveler

9 Colmados
The Dominican institution of the corner-store bar is found in every neighborhood, normally with a well-stocked refrigerator, a television or a steady stream of soothing music.

10 Markets
Although they range from big covered halls to a few stalls on a street corner, markets are a crucial part of social life and a great way to meet local people. You might not want to buy much on show, but the atmosphere makes a visit worthwhile.

Shop at Playa Sosúa

Top 10 Customs & Beliefs

1 Politeness
Old-fashioned Hispanic courtesy is important. For example, greeting those present when entering a room.

2 Dress
Even impoverished Dominicans make a huge effort to look well dressed. Scruffiness is not appreciated.

3 The Church
Almost all Dominicans claim to be Catholics, even though only a small percentage regularly attend church.

4 Brujería
The Dominican term for magic, black or white, which most people believe in.

5 Botánicas
Stores or market stalls selling religious and superstitious icons and potions for use in *brujería (see above)*.

6 Siestas
Although some offices and shops stay open all day, most people like an afternoon nap.

7 Hurrying
Almost unknown, and Dominicans do not like pushy foreigners who do not know how to relax.

8 Punctuality
Flexible, especially in social situations. Nevertheless, buses and tours tend to leave on time.

9 Machismo
Totally ingrained among most men, who like to flirt but want their women to stay safely at home.

10 Politics
Elections every two years keep party rivalry keen, though most are skeptical about politicians' promises.

Left **Mercado Modelo** Right **Stalls selling paintings at Cortacito Beach**

🔟 Shopping

1 Mercado Modelo, Santo Domingo

The capital's biggest and most hectic shopping area is a warren of stalls and booths within a concrete hangar, surrounded by streets crammed with sidewalk vendors. The cornucopia of tourist souvenirs includes Haitian paintings, sculptures, rum, CDs, and exotic items connected with *vodu*. ✎ Map N5 • Av Mella 505 • Open 8am–7pm daily

2 Calle El Conde

Santo Domingo's traffic-free central shopping street is the place for merengue or bachata CDs, cigars or cheap T-shirts, and other bargains. The surrounding side streets are also worth exploring for the many gift and souvenir shops *(see p52)*.

3 Museo Mundo de Ambar, Santo Domingo

Although there are many amber outlets in the Zona Colonial, this is one of the most reputable, selling some beautiful examples of jewelry made from the precious resin. Also on sale are earrings and brooches featuring turquoise larimar. An exhibition explains the process, and there is sometimes a craftsman at work as well. ✎ Map P5 • Arzobispo Meriño 452 • 682 3309 • Open 9am–6pm Mon–Sat

Amber

4 Plaza Central, Santo Domingo

One of a growing number of US-style complexes in uptown Santo Domingo, this cool and spacious center offers a range of clothes stores, leather and jewelry outlets, shoe shops, banks, and a movie theater. There's also a tempting array of snacking opportunities, including pizza, ice cream, and a karaoke bar. ✎ Map J3 • Av 27 de Febrero & Winston Churchill • Open 9am–8pm Mon–Sat daily

5 Librería Thesaurus, Santo Domingo

The capital's modern and attractive bookstore has a great selection of books on the country's history and culture, as well as a wide range of English titles, including some children's books. Browsing is welcomed. An added bonus is the pleasant coffee bar selling drinks, snacks, and delicious smoothies. ✎ Map K3 • Av Abraham Lincoln on corner of Av Sarasota • 508 1114 • Open 9am–9pm Mon–Sat, 10am–3pm Sun

Herbs for sale outside Mercado Modelo

For more information on Librería Thesaurus log on to www.thesaurus.com.do

6 Flea Markets

Sunday mornings see the hustle-bustle of several *mercados de pulgas* in the capital. The outdoor gatherings at the Centro de los Héroes, the bottom of Avenida Luperón, and Avenida 30 de Mayo offer unlikely household implements, occasional antiques, day-to-day clothing, and cheap food.
⊗ *Open 7am–12pm Sun*

7 Calle del Sol

The long, straight street of this commercial center cuts through downtown, lined with old-fashioned department stores, banks, and street stalls. You'll find almost everything including "designer" sunglasses from Haiti *(see p15)*. ⊗ *Map C2*

8 Playa Dorada Plaza, Playa Dorada

The North Coast's biggest shopping mall is a Californian-style collection of retail outlets spread over two floors, with the emphasis on the tourist market. Cigars, cosmetics, and clothes feature prominently.
⊗ *Map C1 • 320 2000*

9 Beach Markets

Big tourist resorts such as Bávaro and Bayahibe often allow small traders to set up informal markets. These are places to find genuine bargains away from the overpriced malls. Look out for rum, music, cheap Haitian art and fabrics *(see p23)*.

10 Colmados

The friendly little corner stores doubling as bars are the place to go for day-to-day items such as drinks, snacks or soap. You might not find much to buy, but you'll find the rum cheaper than in tourist stores *(see p53)*.

Top 10 Buys

1 Amber
The golden resin makes beautiful jewelry, but before buying make sure that the piece is authentic.

2 Larimar
This cool blue mineral is mined in the country and is sold uncut or as jewelry.

3 Cigars
Some aficionados rate hand-rolled Dominican cigars even higher than Cuban and they are certainly better value.

4 Rum
White, golden, or *añejo* (dark and aged), each has its appeal and is much cheaper than at home.

5 Wood Carvings
Bowls and plates made from the hardwood *guayacán* tree are attractively solid and extremely colorful.

6 Taino Artifacts
Not the original ones, of course, but well-crafted repli-cas can be found on sale in museums and gift shops.

7 Carnival Masks
The best known are the multicolored *papier-mâché* devil masks from La Vega, available in Santo Domingo.

8 Haitian Art
Though much of it is mass-produced kitsch, you are likely to fall for a resplendent country scene.

9 CDs
The choice of merengue and bachata albums is bewil-dering. Ask the shop assistant to play a few.

10 Coffee
Some of the best mountain-grown aromatic beans in the Caribbean are sold in vacuum-sealed tins at fairly reasonable prices.

Left & Right **La Atarazana, Santo Domingo**

Restaurants

1 La Résidence, Santo Domingo

This recently restored stone house of the former governor Nicolás de Ovando is now a luxury hotel, offering a romantic gourmet dining experience. The early 16th-century mansion oozes with Spanish colonial history. Savor Mediterranean-style dishes here. ✆ *Map P5 • Calle Las Damas • 685 9955 • Open noon–3pm, 7–11pm daily • $$$$$*

2 El Conuco, Santo Domingo

Dominican food is the specialty at this restaurant, which looks like a rustic dwelling. Opt for the fixed-price buffet, which is more extensive in the evening than at lunchtime, or eat *à la carte*. Dancers and musicians perform in native costume. ✆ *Map M3 • Casimiro de Moya 152 • 686 0129 • Open 11am–3pm, 6–12pm daily • $$*

La Résidence, Hostal Nicolás de Ovando

3 La Atarazana, Santo Domingo

Housed in an old colonial building and known for both local and international dishes, especially seafood, this is a pleasant place to stop for lunch while sightseeing, or for dinner. ✆ *Map P5 • Plaza España • 689 2900 • Open noon–until late daily • $$$*

4 Mesón de la Cava, Santo Domingo

Dine in a great setting – a natural cave, with strategic lighting in tunnels, and antechambers. La Cava is popular for steaks and seafood *(see p76)*. ✆ *Map J4 • Parque Mirador del Sur • 533 2818 • Open 11:30am–5pm, 5:30–12pm daily • $$$$*

5 Rancho Luna Steak House, Santiago

The steaks here are large and juicy, but there are other items on the menu, notably fish, for those who don't like red meat. A piano bar and a fine wine list are a bonus *(see p85)*. ✆ *Map C2 • Carretera Luperón 7.5km • 736 7176 • Open for lunch & dinner • $$$*

6 Blue Moon, Cabarete

Reservation is required for this authentic East Indian restaurant in the countryside. Dinner is served on banana leaves, and diners sit on cushions on the floor. It's fun to go in a group as this enables you to order and sample a wide selection of dishes. ✆ *Map D1 • Los Brazos • 223 0614 • Open noon–12pm daily • $$$*

7 Vesuvio, Santo Domingo

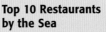

Opened in 1954, this remains one of the best places to go for

Detail on the wall of Vesuvio

an elegant meal. The cuisine is mostly Italian, with delicious seafood and pasta, complemented by dishes from around the Caribbean. ◎ *Map L4 • Av George Washington 521 • 221 1954 • Open noon–3pm, 6pm–until late daily • $$$$$*

8 Pez Dorado, Santiago

A well established bistro, popular with the upper-income residents, particularly for family Sunday lunches and business encounters. The menu is a combination of Chinese, Dominican, and international dishes. The food and wines are excellent, and portions are generous. ◎ *Map C2 • Calle del Sol 43, Santiago de los Caballeros • 582 2518 • Open noon–12pm daily • $$$$*

9 El Café, Santiago

With smart decor and beautifully laid tables, the café is popular with the upper crust of Santiago society. The chef serves up excellent international dishes such as rack of lamb, steaks, and fish. ◎ *Map C2 • Av Texas esq Calle 5, Jardines Metropolitanos, Santiago de los Caballeros • 587 4247 • Lunch–until late • $$$$*

10 Sully, Santo Domingo

A good place for all seafood-lovers, with generous portions of fish, prawns, and other delicacies. Seafood chowder is recommended. The catch of the day is also good and everything is absolutely fresh. ◎ *Map L4 • Av Charles Summer 19 y Calle Caoba, Los Prados • 562 3389 • Open noon–3pm, 7–12pm Tue–Sun • $$$*

Top 10 Restaurants by the Sea

1 Las Salinas
Has a varied menu from substantial burgers to lobster at $10 (see p113).

2 Adrian Tropical, Santo Domingo
A place to try local specialities such as mofongo (see p76).

3 El Paraíso, Playa El Valle
Serves delicious fish and shrimp from a beach shack under palm trees (see p104).

4 Capitán Cook, Bávaro
Choose your own freshly caught lobster or fish at this lively restaurant (see p77).

5 Neptuno's Club, Boca Chica
Seafood restaurant built out over the water with a replica caravel for a bar (see p77).

6 On the Waterfront, Sosúa
Offers glorious views at sunset (see p58).

7 Casa Boga, Las Terrenas
Located in a former fishing village, and serving delicious Basque fish and seafood dishes (see p104).

8 Villa Serena, Las Galeras
The view beyond the gardens, of an islet and a single palm, is romantically lovely (see p133).

9 Lax
Popular with windsurfers and kiteboarders for its Mexican specials and sushi. ◎ *Map D1 • Cabarete • Open 11am–until late • $$$*

10 La Casa del Pescador
Serves fresh fish and seafood including an excellent paella for two. ◎ *Map D1 • Cabarete • 571 0760 • Open noon–11pm daily • $$$$*

Left **Café Cito, Puerto Plata** Right **On the Waterfront sign, Sosúa**

🔟 Bars

1 Atarazana 9, Santo Domingo

Time your sightseeing in the old city so that you can have an evening drink here. It's one of the many historic buildings around the Alcázar de Colón *(see p9)* that have been converted into a bar or restaurant. The bar serves good drinks. ◈ *Map P4 • Zona Colonial • 688 0969 • Open 11am–12pm daily*

2 Beer House, Santo Domingo

The locally brewed Presidente is a great beer for a hot day, but here you can also choose from up to 40 beers from around the world. The atmosphere is casual and friendly, and often there's live music, including jazz. ◈ *Map J2 • Gustavo Mejía Ricart Esquina Av Winston Churchill • 683 4804 • Open 5pm–until late daily*

3 Café Cito, Puerto Plata

Just outside the complex of all-inclusive hotels, this bar is popular with ex-pats, and tourists from nearby resorts. There's a pool table, sports TV screen, live jazz music, and karaoke on weekends. ◈ *Map C1 • Playa Dorada • Open 10:30am–12pm Mon–Sat*

4 Jungle Bar, Puerto Plata

This English-run bar is a favorite with the British crowd. You can get a chip butty (sandwich) or a fried breakfast, and all the usual drinks. There are often

Beer

event nights, when the bar stays open till late. ◈ *Map C1 • Plaza Turisol 12 • 261 3544 • Open 10am–6pm*

5 On the Waterfront, Sosúa

Primarily a restaurant, this bar on the cliff-top overlooking the sea is a great place for a sunset cocktail. ◈ *Map D1 • Calle Dr Rosen 1 • Open 8am–10pm daily • Happy hours 4–6pm*

6 Syroz, Las Terrenas

This famous bar, on the beach by the Pueblo de los Pescadores, has a dance floor where most of the action takes place. Live music on the weekends *(see p105)*. ◈ *Map F2 • 866 5577 • Open 5pm–4am daily*

7 José Oshay's Irish Beach Pub, Cabarete

Walk through José Oshay's shopping village, off the main road, to reach this beachfront bar. Food is available, but it's basically a drinking spot, packed at night with windsurfers burning candles at both ends after a busy day on the waves *(see p91)*. ◈ *Map D1 • 571 0775 • Open 8am–1am daily*

8 Pop Lounge, Santo Domingo

The ambience here is of a European club, but, although there's music, there's no dance floor. The club has several rooms, and bars that are decorated in different colors – a rainbow theme that is continued in the cocktails and ice. ⊛ Map N5 • Arzobispo Nouel esquina Hostos, Zona Colonial • 686 5176 • Open 9pm–until late daily

9 Alta Copa, Santo Domingo

Formerly a wine shop, the Alta Copa has been transformed into a wine bar decorated as a Spanish cava. Cocktails as well as wine are served at this sought-after meeting place for the Dominicans. ⊛ Map J4 • Pedro A Bobea, Bella Vista • 532 6405 • Open 6pm–until late

10 Hemingway's Café, Puerto Plaza

The bar is decorated along the theme of Ernest Hemingway, with nautical and sportfishing paraphernalia around the walls. On weekends there's live music and some karaoke, otherwise a DJ plays rock, Latin electronic, and house music. It's popular with visitors, and tourists from the resorts who want a change of scenery. ⊛ Map C1 • Playa Dorada Shopping Mall • 320 2230 • Open 11am–until late daily

Hemingway's Café, Playa Dorado

Top 10 Drinks

1 Presidente Beer
This deservedly world-famous lager-style brew is usually served so cold that it's almost frozen.

2 Rum
Dominican rum is among the Caribbean's best, and is the national drink (see p55).

3 Ron Ponch
Rum disguised with sweet fruit juices and cordials, and therefore to be treated with extreme caution.

4 Coffee
Locally grown coffee is delicious drunk as a simple espresso, but hotels often offer instant grains.

5 Coconut Milk
Cool coconut milk drunk straight from a freshly chopped nut is the quin-tessential Caribbean thirst quencher.

6 Juices
An infinite variety of tropical fruits (see p65) are turned into irresistible juices, with or without extra sugar.

7 Batidas
Fruit juice mixed in the blender with crushed ice and condensed milk to produce smoothies.

8 Morir Soñando
"To die dreaming" is the poetic name for a blend of orange juice, milk, and ice.

9 Refrescos
The general term for soda-style soft drinks of different colors and degrees of sweetness.

10 Ponche de Frutas
An alcohol-free punch of mixed juices makes a refreshing change from its rum-blended relative.

Left **Las Brisas, Cabarete** Right **Crazy Moon, Puerto Plata**

🔟 Nightlife & Merengue Venues

1 Club 60, Santo Domingo
Attracting the older crowd with classic rock, merengue, and ballads, this club is only open on weekends. On Friday and Saturday you can hear merengue, and on Sundays there's Cuban son for a different Latin beat. ◈ Map L3 • Máximo Gómez 60 • Open 9pm–until late Fri–Sun • Cover charge

2 Guácara Taína, Santo Domingo
Set in a natural cave, this place is decorated with stalactites and Taíno pictographs. There are native dance shows (the club has two dance floors), and fashion shows are also held here (see p75). ◈ Map M3 • Paseo de los Indios, Av Cayetano Germosén • 533 0671 • Open 9pm–2am Tue–Sun

3 Jet Set, Santo Domingo
A casual place where Dominicans come for good Latin dance music. Things don't get going until after midnight and

Jet Set, Santo Domingo

continue till dawn. Look out for live merengue bands on Mondays (see p75) . ◈ Map J4 • Independencia 2253 • 535 4145 • Open 10pm–until late daily

4 Salón La Fiesta, Santo Domingo
One of the top international hotels along the Malecón, offering a variety of nightlife, starting with a piano bar for evening cocktails. The disco usually plays Dominican music. When you're tired of dancing, move on to the casino for a spot of gambling. ◈ Map M4 • Jaragua Hotel • 688 8026 • Open daily until late

5 Alcázar, Santiago
This Spanish restaurant and bar offers meals or tapas, and there is a casino for adult amusement. The real action begins at around 1am when Dominicans, dressed smartly but provocatively, arrive for a good time. ◈ Map C3 • Gran Almirante Hotel & Casino, Estrella Sadhalá esquina Calle, Santiago de los Caballeros 10 • Open 10pm–until late daily

6 Las Brisas, Cabarete
At the east end of the town, on the beach, this lively nightspot offers a reasonably priced Tex Mex buffet. Las Brisas is the only place in Cabarete that plays Dominican music at night – merengue and bachata (see p91). ◈ Map D1 • Calle Principal • 571 0614 • Open 8am–until late, kitchen closes around 10pm

7 D'Classico, Sosúa

A large, fun disco where they play a mixture of merengue, bachata, Latin music, rock, and pop. At weekends

Salsa

it's mainly Dominican music, which attracts local youth keen to befriend foreigners and teach them how to dance (see p91). ⊗ Map D1 • Calle Pedro Clisante • Open 10pm–until late

8 Crazy Moon, Puerto Plata

A bar and disco where DJs entertain with merengue, salsa, and international music. Although most customers are tourists, there are lots of Dominicans around to teach them the dance routines (see p91). ⊗ Map C1 • Paradise Beach Resort, Playa Dorada • 320 3663 • Open 10pm–4am Mon–Sat

9 Aire, Santo Domingo

One of the capital's best gay clubs. Wednesday is the Foam Party, Saturday the Message Party, and on Sunday there's a drag and stripper show. DJs play house and dance music until dawn (see p75). ⊗ Map N5 • Calle Mercedes 313 • 689 4163 • Open 10pm–until late Wed–Sun

10 Loft Lounge & Dance Club, Santo Domingo

A spirited venue, which has attracted some leading merengue bands, including Fernando Villalona and Los Hermanos Rosario, to perform live. Enjoy salsa and international pop music, with DJs spinning disks until everyone crawls off to bed. ⊗ Map K3 • Tiradentes 44, Naco • 732 4016 • Open 10pm–until late

Top 10 Merengue Performers

1 Conjunto Quisqueya
One of the 1970s big bands that has adapted traditional folk rhythms into urban dance music.

2 Fulanito
This band mixes merengue with rap and hip-hop to produce "merenhouse" music.

3 Juan Luis Guerra
An international superstar, the classically trained musician blends jazz-influenced merengue and sentimental bachata music.

4 Milly Quezada
"The Queen of Merengue" has been an internationally popular singer and bandleader since the 1970s.

5 Los Hermanos Rosario
A six-brother boy band from Higüey, which recorded several bestselling albums in its 1980s heyday.

6 Toño Rosario
Formerly of the Hermanos Rosario, Toño, a.k.a. El Cuco, is a modern-day merengue superstar.

7 Luis Segura
Dubbed "the Father of Bachata", the veteran Segura sings the tear-jerking Dominican version of C&W.

8 Cuco Valoy
Prodigiously gifted and versatile musician credited with fusing African and Cuban influences into mainstream merengue.

9 Wilfrido Vargas
Multitalented composer and performer who has popularized merengue across Latin America.

10 Johnny Ventura
An extrovert exponent of brass-dominated dance music.

Left **Bandera Dominicana** Right **Sancocho**

Dishes of the Dominican Republic

1 Bandera Dominicana
The closest thing to a national dish, the so-called Dominican flag doesn't exactly copy the colors of the nation's emblem. But, it does provide a nutritious mix of red beans, rice, shredded beef or chicken, salad and avocado, and fried plantain or boiled yucca. This combination is available everywhere, and is extremely filling.

2 Sancocho
A close relative of stews made in Colombia and Venezuela, real *sancocho* contains no fewer than five different sorts of meat (chicken, goat, pork, beef, and sausage) as well as a medley of vegetables and spices. It's a dish for very special occasions, also reflecting the country's mixed European and African heritage.

Lobster

3 Chivo Asado
The humble goat, seen browsing at every roadside, is a firm favorite, especially when roasted into a state of extreme tenderness after being marinated in rum and spices. This delicacy is normally reserved for holidays and celebrations, when it might be eaten with traditional flat rounds of cassava bread.

4 Lambi
The country's seafood, including sea bass, lobster, and shrimp, is varied and delicious. Of almost legendary status among locals, however, is *lambi* or conch, served cold with a vinaigrette or hot in a tomato and garlic stew. This large mollusk may seem a little chewy, but its appeal lies in its supposedly aphrodisiac qualities.

5 Mangú
A wholesome and extremely satisfying breakfast staple, this has nothing to do with mangoes but is a very filling plate of mashed plantain, drizzled with olive oil and sometimes seasoned with fried onions or cheese. A welcome break from imitation American breakfasts, this will match the largest of morning appetites.

6 Mofongo
Another calorie-laden plantain favourite, this is eaten as a side dish for lunch or dinner. Plantains are fried, mashed, and mixed with garlic and pieces of fried bacon. The delicious end result can be filled with a sauce such as prawns or beef, but it is very good on its own.

7 Mondongo
Not under any circumstances to be confused with *mofongo*, *mondongo* is a formidable dish of pig's tripe, stewed in a tomato and garlic sauce. It has its fans among

Dominicans, especially as a Sunday brunch treat, as it is supposed to help cure the most stubborn of hangovers.

8 Asopao
A Dominican cross between a thick soup, a gumbo, and a Spanish paella, this mix of rice, chicken stock and spices can be served with chicken or seafood. A slightly less liquid version is called *locrio*, again featuring rice, vegetables and your choice of meat or seafood.

9 Casabe
Passed down by the indigenous Tainos, the making of cassava flour involves an intricate process of removing toxic cyanide residues by grating and drying the starch-filled tubers. The flour is then used to make a bread with a hard biscuit-like texture that can be eaten as a side dish or snack.

10 Dulce de Leche
Of all the ultra-sweet desserts beloved by Dominicans, this is by far the most wides-pread, a simple but irresistible blend of whole milk and sugar stirred together over a low heat until it reaches a cream-like consistency. Look out for variations on this sweet-toothed theme involving coconut and candied fruits.

Asopao

Top 10 Snacks

1 Pastelitos
Small but tasty pasties or turnovers filled with a savoury center of minced beef, chicken or cheese.

2 Empanadas
A similar deep-fried turnover filled with meat or cheese but here it is made with yucca flour.

3 Quipes
Another standard street snack, featuring Middle East-inspired cracked wheat rissoles stuffed with meat.

4 Yaniqueques
A local distortion of Johnny Cakes, this version is a sort of fried round corn bread served hot.

5 Chicharones
Deep-fried pieces of crunchy pork rind or crackling, sometimes chicken pieces are also used.

6 Chimichurris
A more hearty snack of slices of pork cut from a joint and eaten in a sandwich.

7 Batatas
Baked sweet potatoes are cooked over embers and scooped out of the skin. Can be eaten either hot or cold.

8 Fritos Maduros
A Dominican version of fries, these are chunks of deep-fried ripe plantain, sprinkled with a little salt.

9 Tostones
Fried plantains again, but of the unripe type and more savoury, fried once, flattened, and refried.

10 Coconut Water
Drunk through a hole in the soft green coconut and sold almost everywhere, this is an incredibly refreshing drink to beat the heat.

left **Trunk of the mahogany tree** Right **Bougainvillea**

Trees & Flowers

1 Mahogany

This valuable, hard, red-brown wood has been logged and exported ever since the Spanish first established a colony here. It is quite rare in most parts, but you can still see plenty of *caoba* trees, some up to 60-ft (18-m) high, in the Cordillera Central.

2 Hispaniolan Royal Palm

The elegant royal palm is found throughout the island. Measuring up to 60 ft (18 m), its graceful appearance is matched by its usefulness. It provides coconuts as well as wood for house building and its leaves can be used for waterproof thatches.

3 Calabash

A small evergreen tropical tree with a strange nocturnal love life, the calabash's flowers bloom only at night, when they are pollinated by bats. The fruits that develop in clusters along the trunk and branches have a hard green wooden shell, which since Taino times has been used as a utensil and ornament.

4 Creolean Pine

The only pine widespread in the Caribbean, this tree flourishes at altitudes above 6,500 ft (1,981 m), as on the flanks of Pico Duarte. The dense forests of the interior are filled with their distinctive fresh odor, creating an illusion of the Alps in the tropics.

Calabash tree

5 Sea Grape

Ubiquitous along the wilder beaches, this tough shrub looks twisted and stunted but thrives in the inhospitable terrain of sand and salt water. Some grow tall and provide a welcome shade. The so-called grapes, though edible, are extremely sour and taste better when made into a jelly.

6 Orchid

Orchids are big business around Jarabacoa and Constanza, where they are grown commercially for the North American market. The beautiful flowers also grow profusely in the wild, especially in the humid climate of the higher reaches of the Parque Nacional Sierra de Baoruco, where there are over 150 species.

7 Bromeliad

A large grouping of eye-catching plants, of which the pineapple is a member, and increasingly popular as exotic indoor ornamentals. Here, they grow wild, either in the ground or sprouting from a tree, shrub, or even from a telegraph post.

Bougainvillea

8 The bright red, purple or pink flowers of this spectacular shrub are in fact, large bracts that surround the small and inconspicuous flowers. A great favorite as a garden plant because it flowers for most of the year, it is actually a native of South America and was imported to the Caribbean.

Hortensia

9 Also a common female name in the Dominican Republic, the mop-headed hortensia is a very popular plant, having been imported from Japan. Such is the quantity of these flowers growing around the central town of Bonao that it is widely known as the Villa de las Hortensias.

Prickly Pear Cactus

10 One of the many types of spiny plants that cling precariously to life in the parched desert regions around Barahona and Monte Cristi is the *opuntia*, known among the locals as *tuna*. It produces pretty flowers on its plump water-retaining pads before the pinkish and very hard-to-handle fruits appear. The inhabitants of the Dominican Republic consider the flesh quite a delicacy.

Hortensia or hydrangea

Top 10 Fruits

Guineo
1 The local name for bananas, but unlike the large starchy plantains the *guineos* are the smaller and sweeter variety.

Lechoza
2 The very popular and succulent papaya or papaw, normally served with banana at breakfast.

Guanábana
3 A variety of sugar apple or *sweetsop*, its sweet white flesh tastes rather like vanilla.

Jagua
4 This light brown fruit with a distinctive sweet taste is a member of the sugary custard-apple family.

Caimito
5 A star apple. The round, usually yellow fruit contains a sweet, sticky pulp.

Mamey
6 The brown-skinned mamey-apple has orange, red, or reddish-brown flesh that makes an amazingly appetizing *batida*.

Zapote
7 The flesh of the zapote tastes like a cross between a banana and a peach.

Piña
8 The familiar pineapple is locally grown and is a firm favorite not only in milkshakes but also at buffets.

Chinola
9 This is a Dominican term for the passion fruit. Though rich in vitamins, it requires a spoonful of sugar to balance its sharpness.

Tamarindo
10 The tamarind's mushy flesh tastes bitter when raw, but is often cooked and used to make delicious drinks.

65

American crocodile at Lago Enriquillo

Animal Life

American Crocodile
Up to 15 ft (4.5 m) in length, these crocs can look fearsome, but are in fact much more timid than their African or Australian relatives. They live up to 50 years on a diet of fish, waterfowl, and small mammals, thriving in the protected salt-water environment of Lago Enriquillo.

Rhinoceros Iguana
The big lizard up to 4-ft (1.2-m) long gets its name from a horn-like bump on its nose. Naturally shy, they have become used to humans on the Isla Cabritos *(see p26)*, but normally seek refuge from the heat in burrows. They bask in the sun to become active and live on very sparse vegetation.

Leatherback Turtle
An endangered species, the leatherback has no shell, but rather a series of bony plates covered with a leathery skin. These creatures can be over 6 ft (1.8 m) and weigh some

Iguana

800 lb (363 kg). They lay hundreds of eggs on remote beaches but are illegally hunted for meat and eggs.

Solenodon
You won't see one of these long-nosed ant-eating mammals in the wild, as they are rare, extremely shy, and nocturnal. They are also now a threatened species, largely because their habitat is shrinking, and they are easy prey for dogs and other predators. A few can still be seen in captivity.

Hutia
Another shy mammal, the endemic *hutia* looks rather like a rat, but it's actually a rabbit-sized herbivore that seeks refuge either in caves or in trees. Increasingly endangered by deforestation, it lives in the more remote and forested districts of the Parque Nacional del Este *(see p41)* and the Parque Nacional Los Haitises *(see p33)*.

Lizard
Reptiles of all shapes and sizes have adapted to the island's varied ecosystems. The diverse variety of the species ranges from the hefty 4-ft (1.2-m) iguanas and chunky geckos to the tiny 1.6-cm jaragua gecko which was discovered in 1998 on the isolated Isla Beata of the southwest coast. Don't be surprised to have a lizard or two visit your room.

7 Tree Frog

Popular among the locals as a *coqui*, the tiny greenish-brown frog is one of several similar species known for their surprisingly loud choruses during the hours of darkness. One of the most evocative of Caribbean sounds, the tireless nocturnal singing of tree frogs becomes louder after a heavy downpour.

Tree frog

8 Whale

Samaná Bay and the Banco de la Plata (Silver Bank), areas some 60-miles (97-km) north of Puerto Plata, are the preferred mating and calving grounds of humpback whales, which can grow up to a staggering 50 ft (15 m) and weigh 40 tons. It is a delight to see them leap out of the water.

9 Manatee

The rare and protected sea cow is the gentle giant of the ocean. Shy and vegetarian, it can reach 12 ft (3.6 m) in length, and rises to the sea's surface every five minutes to breathe air. It's hard to believe that this bulbous and whiskery creature was once mistaken for a mermaid.

10 Butterflies

Almost 300 species of butterfly have been identified, but it is thought there are many more, especially in the remote mountain terrain of the Sierra de Baoruco. The arid southwest is home to hundreds of colorful species, including some rare swallowtails and monarchs, attracting growing numbers of lepidopterists.

Top 10 Birds

1 Hispaniolan Woodpecker

Known as the *carpintero*, this handsome yellow and brown bird is unique to the island.

2 Hispaniolan Parakeet

Though an endangered species, it is instantly recognizable from its bright green feathers with red patches.

3 Hispaniolan Emerald Hummingbird

Found in the mountainous interior, the female species is lighter in hue than the black-breasted male.

4 Hispaniolan Trogon

A multicolored little bird, with gray breast, red belly, green back, and a black-and-white tail.

5 Cattle Egret

The heron-like white bird can be seen in almost every field, and especially around flea-ridden cattle.

6 Turkey Vulture

No great beauty with its bare red face, it is nevertheless a useful carrion eater.

7 Flamingo

Pink and elegant in flight, this is the most attractive of the country's many estuary and lagoon birds.

8 Palm Chat

The brown *sigua palmera* is the national bird, nesting high up in the foliage of a palm tree.

9 Red-tailed Hawk

The versatile and efficient raptor that feeds on small mammals and reptiles is actually a buzzard.

10 Frigate Bird

This magnificent coal-black sea bird has a red throat that expands dramatically during its mating rituals.

AROUND THE DOMINICAN REPUBLIC

DOMINICAN REPUBLIC'S TOP 10

Left **The Malecón, Santo Domingo** Center **Los Tres Ojos** Right **Boca Chica Beach**

Santo Domingo & the South Coast

FROM THE BUSTLING CAPITAL CITY to the huge expanses of beach that make up the Costa del Coco, the Dominican Republic's South Coast is an intriguing mix of tourist activity and natural beauty. The southeast contains the country's traditional sugar territory, with huge plantations stretching to the horizon. This is also the heartland of baseball culture, centered around La Romana and San Pedro de Macorís, where local kids dream of making it big in the United States. Some of the country's most established seaside resorts are here, as well as the modern complexes of Bávaro and Punta Cana, offering a choice of quiet swimming or crowded people-watching. Most of the coastline can be reached by the scenic Carretera 3, which runs adjacent to the sea, but the remote wilderness of the Parque Nacional del Este is only accessible by boat.

Statue of Fray Montesino,
Santo Domingo

🔟 Sights

1	Santo Domingo	**6**	San Pedro de Macorís
2	Los Tres Ojos	**7**	La Romana
3	Acuario Nacional	**8**	Bayahibe
4	Boca Chica	**9**	Parque Nacional del Este
5	Juan Dolio	**10**	Costa del Coco

Santo Domingo

1 La Capital has something for everyone, whether cobbled colonial-era streets steeped in history or state-of-the-art shopping malls. A patchwork of ancient and modern, the sprawling city lives life at a frantic pace, with gridlocked streets and other urban challenges. But there are quiet corners and shady plazas in the Zona Colonial, extensive parks offering fresh air, peace, and quiet, and the magnificent seaside Malecón, the favorite playground of Santo Domingo's inhabitants *(see pp8–11)*.

Los Tres Ojos

2 The Three Eyes are a complex of *cenotes* or karst caves containing a subterranean mini-lagoon and stalactites and stalagmites. What appears to be four lakes is, in fact, a single one, taking different colors under different lights in four caverns. Steps lead steeply down to the first cave, from where walkways and a pulley-powered vessel take visitors through the

Boaters at Los Tres Ojos

underground system. Reputedly a Taino holy site, the place is surprisingly unspoilt despite large numbers of tourists, and the last of the "eyes" offers a spectacular natural landscape of tropical vegetation, sheer rock faces, and green-tinged water.
 Map E4 • Av Las Américas • Open 9am–5pm daily • Adm

Acuario Nacional

3 This technically impressive installation uses natural seawater to fill its various tanks, displaying an enormous and colorful range of tropical marine life. The pride of this place is Tamaury, an orphaned manatee, which was saved in 1995 after its mother was killed and now basks, apparently quite happily, in a large tank. A pleasant snack bar looks over the sea *(see p36)*.

Boca Chica

4 The easiest beach to reach from Santo Domingo is a boisterous and unpretentious place, verging on the raucous at weekends when tens of thousands of people escape from the capital to swim and listen to music. During the week it's a lot quieter, but even then there's no shortage of bars and restaurants. There are a number of hotels and guesthouses, too, offering good-value accommodation. The main draw is the beach *(see p37)*, a lovely strip of sand set in a protective bay with clear water.

Stalactite formation in Los Tres Ojos caves

Left **Playa Juan Dolio** Right **Victorian houses along the Malecón, San Pedro de Macorís**

5 Juan Dolio

This long strip of hotels and guesthouses set on the coast is not really a town as such, but an extended tourist enclave. Dating from the 1980s, when investors saw the potential of a new resort on the South Coast, it features mostly modern architecture and well-designed hotels. Most of the action revolves around the beaches, which range from the fairly rocky to the sublimely sandy. The latter are normally situated by the larger all-inclusive hotels, where different water sports are on offer. ◈ Map F4

6 San Pedro de Macorís

A city's whose fortunes have ebbed and flowed with world sugar prices, San Pedro was once the richest place in the country. Some of its Victorian buildings, such as the fire station and the mansions near the Parque Duarte, recall the boom years. But those times have gone – just a memory since San Pedro was battered by Hurricane Georges in 1998. Nowadays, the city produces world-class baseball players, some descended from the English-speaking migrants called cocolos, who settled on the island at the turn of the 19th century. ◈ Map F4

7 La Romana

This town boasts some pretty houses from the turn of the 19th century in the gridiron area around the Parque Central, as well as a large, sprawling market area where you will see all manner of everyday and exotic produce. The town is famed for its baseball players, but its real attractions for visitors are the nearby luxury resort of Casa de Campo and the unique replica Tuscan hilltop village of Altos de Chavón (see pp24–25).

8 Bayahibe

Until the 1990s this was a quiet fishing village, with nothing much more than a few boats pulled up on the beach. But a wave of tourist development has changed its character, bringing more amenities and many more visitors. Even so, the

Cocolo Heritage

The descendants of cocolos, who came to San Pedro from British Caribbean territories such as Tortola and Anguilla, still celebrate their heritage at the annual Fiesta of San Pedro, in June, with dancing and fancy costumes. The festivities are thought to derive from traditional English Christmas mummers' rituals involving miming and disguises.

pastel-colored wooden huts and gracious palm trees that line the beach still form a pretty scene, while the jetty is the starting point for boat trips to the offshore Isla Saona and Isla Catalina. Bayahibe is also well endowed with eating and drinking spots. ◎ *Map G4*

9 Parque Nacional del Este
Adjacent to the well-trodden tourist track of Bayahibe and Playa Dominicus, this large expanse of protected natural wilderness covers over 100,000 acres of dry forest and palm-ined beaches. The terrain on the mainland peninsula is much tougher going and less popular with tourists, but offers the determined explorer a wealth of birdlife and tropical vegetation as well as glimpses of Taino art and culture *(see p41)*.

10 Costa del Coco
The southeast tip of the country is everyone's idea of a desert island idyll – a sweeping panorama of soft sand and gently swaying palm trees facing a turquoise sea. Mass tourism may have brought many thousands of visitors each year to the complexes of Punta Cana and Bávaro, but even the arrival of all-inclusive hotels has done little to affect the majesty of this coastline *(see pp22–23)*.

Bayahibe

South Coast Drive

Morning

🕐 Leave congested Santo Domingo in a rental car after spending an hour admiring the sharks and manatee at the seaside **Acuario Nacional**. You could have a late breakfast or snack in the aquarium's cafeteria. A half-hour or so driving along the well-maintained Carretera 3, which passes the airport, brings you to the resort of **Boca Chica**. Take a look at its famous beach a few blocks to your right, traffic allowing, and have lunch at one of the many beachside shacks selling fish, conch, or shrimps.

Afternoon

Passing eastwards through tourist developments such as Juan Dolio and flat stretches of agricultural land, you reach **San Pedro de Macorís**, where you might take a look at some of the Victorian-era buildings. Or press on to **La Romana** for a quick tour of the old quarter around the **Parque Central** *(see p24)*.

🕐 If returning to Santo Domingo, there's enough time to drive up to **Altos de Chavón** *(see p25)*, the replica Tuscan village with designer boutiques and fantastic views over the river valley. Head back towards the capital, allowing a couple of hours before night falls.

Or drive back to the coastal road and turn left towards Bayahibe, where you can spend the night in one of the inexpensive hotels (advance booking necessary) or the beachside complexes along Playa Viva Dominicus.

Left & Center **Isla Saona, Parque Nacional del Este** Right **Casa Ponce de León**

Best of the Rest

1 Parque Mirador del Este
On the east bank of the Ozama, overlooked by the imposing Faro a Colón, this stretch of open parkland has a fine selection of trees and makes for a pleasant walk. ✆ *Map E4*

2 La Caleta Submarine Park
The main attraction for scuba divers and snorkelers is the *Hickory* wreck, deliberately sunk here, as well as coral reefs which are accessible from the Park's beach. ✆ *Map E4* • 472 4204 • Open 9am–6pm daily • Adm

Playa Guayacanes

3 Playa Guayacanes
A quieter alternative to Boca Chica *(see p71)*, the long strip of soft sand and calm water, still home to a fishing community, attracts a mix of tourists and locals. ✆ *Map F4*

4 Tetelo Vargas Baseball Stadium
This concrete temple to the great Dominican passion is usually open during the day. ✆ *Map F4* • Av Circunvalación, San Pedro • 246 4077

5 Playa Boca del Soco
The best beach in the San Pedro de Macorís area *(see p72)*, it marks the point where the Río Soco meets the sea. It also offers swimming in both salt and fresh water. ✆ *Map F4*

6 Río Soco River Trip
A couple of tour operators organize trips up this wide river near San Pedro, during which you pass idyllic palm-lined meadows and pretty wooded hillsides. ✆ *Map G4 • Student Services: 937 0421*

7 Isla Saona
The most popular part of Parque Nacional del Este *(see p73)* can be easily reached by regular boat services. Despite the crowds, the island looks like a Robinson Crusoe fantasy. ✆ *Map G5* • Tropical Tours: 523 3333

8 Casa de Ponce de León
The squat, fortified stone house, built in 1505, belonged to Ponce de León, founder of Puerto Rico and Florida. ✆ *Map H4* • Open 9am–5pm Mon–Sat • Adm

9 Higüey
The sprawling modern city is nothing special, but the basilica *(see p49)*, built to replace the much older Iglesia San Dionisio, is certainly impressive. ✆ *Map G4*

10 La Otra Banda
This sleepy one-street village is popular with Costa del Coco *(see pp22–3)* excursionists, largely because of its bright and photogenic wooden houses, built by immigrants from the Canary Islands. ✆ *Map G4*

For further information on tour operators, log onto www.studentservicesdr.freeservers.com or www.tropicaltourssa.com

Jet Set, Santo Domingo

Price Categories

For a three-course meal
and a beer for one
including tax and
service.

$	under $10
$$	$10–$20
$$$	$20–$30
$$$$	$30–$40
$$$$$	over $40

Nightlife

1 Fusion Rose
Midweek hip-hop electronic music with DJ Mahogany makes this a very popular spot with a young Dominican crowd.
◈ *Map P5 • El Conde esq Las Damas, Zona Colonial, Santo Domnigo • 449 2346 • Cover charge*

2 Guácara Taína
The premier club of Santo Domingo is in a beautifully lit cave located about 98-ft (30-m) underground. Bands often perform live, and there are merengue workshops for foreigners *(see p60)*.

3 Jet Set
A great place in Santo Domingo for both recorded and live Latin music – mostly traditional. Juan Luís Guerra songs are always played *(see p60)*.

4 Salón La Fiesta
With a capacity of 1,400, this is one of the main venues in the capital for hosting live bands. However it's mainly used as a disco *(see p60)*.

5 Aire
The leading gay club in Santo Domingo, Aire hosts popular theme nights, and lots of parties, and plays music from the 1970s and 80s *(see p61)*.

6 Monetecristo Café
Named after the Count of Monte Cristo, this English-style pub and café offers hot and cold snacks. ◈ *Map J2 • Calle José Amado Soler esquina Abraham Lincoln, Santo Domingo • 542 5000 • Open 6pm–5am daily*

7 Secreto Musical Bar
Latin music with merengue, salsa, and bachata ballads are played, but, most importantly, this is the headquarters of the Club Nacional de los Soneros, so there's lots of Cuban music, particularly son. ◈ *Map N2 • Baltazar de los Reyes esquina Pimentel, Santo Domingo • Open evenings until late*

8 Barceló Bávaro Casino
Five Barceló hotels share the facilities of a 24-hour casino, a theater featuring Las Vegas-style Tropicalísimo casino shows, and a disco which plays a variety of music. ◈ *Map H4 • Bávaro, Higüey • Disco: midnight–4am*

9 Hamaca Coral by Hilton
At this venue, the music's mostly Latin. American and English numbers are played occasionally. A well-equipped casino with tables and slot machines awaits those who enjoy gambling. ◈ *Map F4 • Boca Chica • Open 11pm–4am*

10 Seven to Seven
A disco with an up-beat atmosphere, Seven plays a lot of techno, but you may also dance to salsa, merengue, and international music. ◈ *Map M4 • Av George Washington 165, Santo Domnigo • 689 2911 • Open 7pm–7am*

Left & Center **Mesón de la Cava** Right **Adrian Tropical**

TOP 10 Restaurants, Santo Domingo

1 Coco's
A charming English-pub-style bar and restaurant serving curried lamb and rice, chicken liver and chips, accompanied by fine wines or English ales.
⊗ Map P6 • Padre Billini 53 • 687 9624 • Open noon–3pm, 6:30–10:30 Tue–Sat, noon–3pm Sun • $$$

2 Mesón de Barí
Mesón offers excellent Dominican cuisine with typical local dishes. ⊗ Map M3 • Hostos esquina Arzobispo Nouel • 687 4091 • Open noon–1am • $$

3 Taboo Bamboo
Try the vodka-based Absolut Tambo Bamboo cocktail, as a change from rum. They also host music festivals and live music shows. ⊗ Map K2 • Roberto Pastoriza 313 Tiradentes y Lope de Vega • 227 2727 • Open for lunch & dinner • $$$

4 Mesón de la Cava
Relish the experience of dining on delicious seafood inside a spectacular natural cave (see p56).

5 Aqua Sushi Bar
Good Japanese fusion food for lunch or dinner. ⊗ Map J2 • Av Abraham Lincoln esq Gustavo M Ricart, Plaza Rosa • 540 3116 • Open noon–12pm • $$

6 La Briciola
A lovely colonial courtyard and terrace provides the perfect setting for dinner by candlelight. Italian cuisine is the speciality.
⊗ Map P6 • Arzobispo Merino 152 • 688 5055 • Open 6pm–late • $$$$

7 Museo de Jamón
Not a museum as the name suggests, but a great Spanish restaurant serving delicious tapas. ⊗ Map P5 • La Atarazana 17 • 688 9644 • Open noon–11pm • $$$$

8 Adrian Tropical
Local dishes such as mofongo, and international cuisine, in an attractive setting by the sea.
⊗ Map M4 • Av George Washington • 221 1764 • Open noon–11pm • $$

9 Lumi's Park
Extremely popular with Dominicans, who like their meat. Good churrasco and tasty mofongo, and lots of local dishes too. They also deliver. ⊗ Map J3 • Av Abraham Lincoln 809 • 540 4755, delivery 540 4584 • Open 8am–12pm • $$

10 Conde de Peñalba
This is a great place for the special local dish, la bandera Dominicana. ⊗ Map P6 • Calle El Conde esquina Arzobispo Meriño • 688 7121 • Open all day • $$

Price Categories

For a three-course meal and a beer for one including tax and service.

$	under $10
$$	$10–$20
$$$	$20–$30
$$$$	$30–$40
$$$$$	over $40

La Casita, La Romana

🍽️ Restaurants, South Coast

1 Neptuno's Club
Set right by the sea, with its dining area built out over the water. The bar is a replica caravel. Excellent fresh fish and seafood *(see p57)*. 🔊 *Map F4 • Boca Chica • 523 4707 • Open 9am–10:30 Tue–Sun • $$$$*

2 Capitán Cook
A restaurant set on the sand in a shady spot under trees. Very popular for lobster (sold by weight), fish, paella and a jug of sangría, for a Spanish touch *(see p57)*. 🔊 *Map H4 • Playa El Cortecito, Bávaro • 552 1061 • Open daily • $$$*

3 La Loma
Clinging to the hillside, with panoramic views, this hotel is difficult to get to, but good for both snacks and meals. 🔊 *Map G3 • Miches • 558 5562 • Open for breakfast, lunch, & dinner • $$*

4 Alisios Bávaro
A hotel restaurant set by a pool, serving Mexican food four days of the week and Thai food the other three. 🔊 *Map H4 • Bávaro, Higüey • 688 1612 • Open for breakfast, lunch, & dinner • $$$*

5 Boca Yate
This French-owned small hotel with a restaurant and bar specializes in fresh lobster and seafood. It's popular with guests from the all-inclusive hotel opposite. 🔊 *Map G4 • Av Eladia Bayahibe, Bayahibe • 688 6822 • Open for dinner until 1am • $$$*

6 Café del Sol
A good lunch spot serving pizzas, salads, and ice creams, set in an amazing location by St. Stanislaus Church and overlooking the Río Chavón *(see p25)*. 🔊 *Map G4 • Altos de Chavón, La Romana • Open for lunch & dinner • $$$*

7 El Sombrero
A Mexican restaurant, complete with Mariachi trio to serenade you as you dine on tortillas and tacos, and sip frozen margaritas. 🔊 *Map G4 • Altos de Chavón, La Romana • Only open at night, reservations required • $$$$*

8 La Casita
The proprietors serve Italian and international cuisine, and specialize in seafood and pasta. The walls are impressively adorned with plates. 🔊 *Map G4 • Francisco R Doucu Dray 57, La Romana • 556 5932 • Open for lunch & dinner • $$$$*

9 DaNancy
Nancy, the owner and chef, cooks delicious lobster and shrimp. Choose your own appetizer from the buffet table. 🔊 *Map F4 • Boca Chica, near La Hamaca Hotel • Open for lunch & dinner • $$*

10 Langosta del Caribe
Lobster and shrimp are big here, cooked on the grill and served indoors or outside under shade. 🔊 *Map H4 • Cortecito 51, Bávaro • 552 0774 • Open for lunch & dinner • $$$*

Following pages **View of mountains from Pico Duarte**

Left **La Vega** Right **Mercado Modelo, Santiago**

The Central Highlands

ENTIRELY DIFFERENT IN TEMPERATURE *and atmosphere from the low-level capital and seaside resorts, the country's interior is dominated by the rugged mountain range known as the Cordillera Central, which arcs down from the Haitian border towards San Cristóbal. The highest point of the range is the Pico Duarte at 10,128 ft (3,087 m), but there are many other peaks and adjacent valleys, especially in and around the popular tourist bases of Jarabacoa and Constanza. Here, you can even feel the chill of an early morning frost, while a profusion of flowers and vegetables thrive in the temperate climate. Santiago is situated within easy reach of the mountains, separating them from the fertile farmland of the Cibao Valley, and from here it is a fascinating excursion westwards through the Highlands to the hilltop town of San José de las Matas.*

Exhibit, Museo de Arte, Bonao

🔟 Sights

1 Bonao	**6** La Ciénega
2 La Vega	**7** San José de las Matas
3 Santo Cerro	**8** San Juan de la Maguana
4 Santiago	**9** Coral de los Indios
5 The Dominican Alps	**10** Las Matas de Farfán

Bonao

1 A place historically dominated by mining, Bonao is not the prettiest site in the country, though it is strategically situated on the Autopista Duarte that connects Santo Domingo to Santiago. The Falconbridge plant, when operating, can be visited free of charge, but also explore the pretty mountain scenery around the town by taking the small road towards the Presa Alto Yuna, the nearby dammed lake. There are fine views of the Cordillera Central. Map D3

La Vega

2 One of the earliest European settlements, La Vega was an important base for gold-mining in the Cibao Valley during Columbus's time, but was later flattened by an earthquake. The modern town reveals nothing of that period. There's little either of Victorian-era boom time, when some imposing public buildings appeared. The most conspicuous structure these days is the concrete modernist Catedral de la Concepción de La Vega, apparently intended to capture the spirit of the colonial period. La Vega really comes into its own each February, when it stages one of the country's most celebrated Carnival celebrations *(see p50)*, and the construction of masks from papier-mâché becomes an art form. Map D2

La Vega

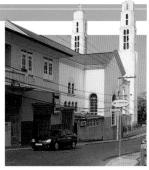

Santiago's cathedral

Santo Cerro

3 Commanding a spectacular view of the valley that Columbus dubbed La Vega Real (Royal Valley), the 19th-century church of Santo Cerro reputedly marks the spot where the Virgin made a miraculous intervention in 1495. The cross that she defended from burning by the Tainos was, according to legend, erected on the hillside by Columbus himself, and the church claims to preserve a fragment of the original crucifix. It's surrounded by ornate Catholic iconography *(see p46)*.

Santiago

4 Smaller and slower paced than the capital, Santiago is nonetheless a major metropolis of over 750,000 people, with contrasting elements of wealth and poverty, old and new. The plush modern suburbs to the north are pleasant, but the city's real atmosphere and interest are concentrated in a relatively small downtown district around the Parque Duarte and the huge Monumento a los Héroes de la Restauracíon, joined by the main shopping street. It's also worth looking into Santiago's proud past as a major producer of sugar and tobacco, especially with a visit to a cigar factory or rum distillery *(see pp14–15)*.

5 The Dominican Alps

This is an ideal place for outdoor activities, ranging from hiking and horseback riding to challenging river-based sports, and the resorts of Jarabacoa and Constanza specialize in excursions. The climate and lack of urban spread also contribute to a wide and varied range of fauna and flora, making it a paradise for bird-watchers and botanists *(see pp12–13)*.

View of Pico Duarte from La Ciénega

6 La Ciénega

The tiny rural village of La Ciénega de Manaboa is the starting point for the popular hike to the summit of Pico Duarte. The office for Parque Nacional Armando Bermúdez *(see p13)* is situated to the north of the village, and it is obligatory to register here and hire a guide. There is a rudimentary camping ground by the park office, where some climbers spend the night before setting off early the next morning. The Ciénega Trail is about 28 miles (45 kms) and usually takes a minimum of three days. ◎ *Map C3*

7 San José de las Matas

Another starting point for a Pico Duarte ascent, this airy and laid-back mountain town provides a fascinating insight into everyday agricultural life. The surrounding countryside is dotted with coffee plantations and small farms, and the town itself acts as a trading center for local farmers. Apart from the *fiesta patronal*, staged every August, you can go on plenty of pleasant excursions to nearby rivers and swimming spots. The town also offers spectacular views over densely wooded hillsides and valleys, dotted with palm trees. ◎ *Map C2*

Ripped Parrot

The strangely named *perico ripao* (ripped parrot) is a style of meringue music developed in Santiago in the early 20th century. With lewd lyrics and an irresistible rhythm, it was frowned upon by polite society. Not surprisingly perhaps, as the Ripped Parrot was the name of a particularly notorious brothel.

8 San Juan de la Maguana

A surprisingly large town lying in a fertile valley to the south of the Cordillera Central, San Juan is a busy agricultural center, surrounded by banana plantations and coffee farms. Its proximity to the Haitian border has brought problems over the centuries as invading armies occupied and destroyed the town. Today's architecture is modern, but there are also some turn-of-the-19th-century buildings around the Parque Central *(see p52)*, where a permanent buzz of outdoor buying and selling makes for an interesting walk. ◎ *Map B3*

Statue of San Juan de la Magauna

Las Matas de Farfán

9 Coral de los Indios

Reputed to be the site of an ancient Taino city, a large open space contains a ring of boulders with what seems to be a ceremonial slab in the middle. It was here that Anacaona, the legendary widow of Caonabo — who was tricked into captivity by the Spanish — attempted to galvanize anti-Spanish feeling among the differing Taino chieftains into a revolt. She was captured and executed, and the settlement destroyed. From what remains it is not clear how much is reconstructed, but the carved stone face on the slab looks authentic enough. ◈ Map B3

10 Las Matas de Farfán

The archetypal Dominican market town, Las Matas (literally roots) is supposed to be named after the tree under which the 18th-century merchant Farfán used to enjoy a siesta. It's still a sleepy sort of place, except on Saturdays when the market brings crowds of *campesinos* into town for some bartering and gossip. There are few tourist sights as such, but Las Matas, as well as the surrounding countryside, gives a taste of small-town rural life. ◈ Map B3

A Morning in Santiago

🕐 After breakfast in your hotel, head for the **Parque Duarte** (see p14), the main downtown hub of activity. It's worth taking a look at some of the grand buildings lining the square, notably the Moorish-style **Centro de Recreo** and the **Palacio Consistorial** (see p14), a gingerbread-style building housing exhibitions. You can also hire a horse-drawn carriage, which should cost no more than $10 for half an hour. Always negotiate a price before setting off.

The carriages normally run down the busy shopping street of **Calle del Sol** (see p55), but you may prefer to walk the mile or so down this buzzing commercial thoroughfare. On the intersection of Calle del Sol and Avenida España you'll come across the **Mercado Modelo**, a cornucopia of tourist souvenirs.

As you reach the end of Calle del Sol and approach the **Monumento a los Héroes de la Restauración** (see p15), you'll certainly have earned a rest and a cold drink. Look out for a couple of bars, such as **Puerto del Sol**.

When you've gathered your strength, it's time to visit the massive monument to the dictator Trujillo (later re-branded as a memorial to independence fighters). The lift has stopped working, so it's a long, rather tiring, climb to the observation platform at the top. But the exertion is worth it for the view, and it'll make you feel better about having lunch.

Mangrove swamps, Parque Nacional del Este

Outdoor Activities

1 Hiking
The Dominican Alps (see pp12–13 & 82) are the perfect place for walking, whether short strolls or hikes. Most hotels can recommend a specialist operator for the more ambitious.

2 Horseback Riding
The region is well equipped for riding enthusiasts, with several outfits such as Rancho Baiguate offering top-class facilities. ⓢ Rancho Baiguate: Map C3 • 574 6890 • www.ranchobaiguate.com.do

White-water rafting near Jarabacoa

3 Cycling
Whether on or off road, cyclists will enjoy fantastic views as well as a warm welcome in villages, where you can always buy drinks.

4 Bird-Watching
The Cordillera Central is home to a number of exotic species, especially in the national parks. Look out for parrots and parakeets, as well as the Hispaniolan woodpecker and the emerald hummingbird.

5 White-Water Rafting
The fast-flowing Río Yaque del Norte near Jarabacoa (see p12) is a favorite place for this adrenaline-fueled sport, involving a fast descent through rocky canyons on a rubber raft shared by several paddlers. ⓢ Franz's Aventuras del Caribe: 574 2669 • www.hispaniola.com/whitewater

6 Kayaking
The Río Yaque del Norte and the Jimenoa (see p13) are good kayaking rivers, with a mix of white water, sharp turns, and precipitous drops. ⓢ Get Wet: Map C3 • Jarabacoa • 586 1170.

7 Canyoning
Jimenoa is the place for this energetic and alarming sport, which involves holding onto a rope and jumping down a sheer rock face into the water below.

8 Cascading
In this variant on canyoning, the participant jumps through a waterfall into the pool at the bottom. The Salto de Jimenoa is a recommended spot.

9 Tubing
The low-budget version of rafting uses a large rubber ring. Swimmers are swept down the river, protected to some degree by the inflated tube.

10 Swimming
This can be enjoyed on the quieter stretches of the Cordillera Central's rivers as well as in many balnearios or swimming holes (see p42).

Price Categories

For a three-course meal and a beer for one person including tax and service charges.

$	under $10
$$	$10–$20
$$$	$20–$30
$$$$	$30–$40
$$$$$	over $40

Guinea fowl, a dish served in Vistabella Club Bar & Grill

Places to Eat & Drink

1 Vistabella Club Bar & Grill
Popular with Dominicans at weekends for its pool, bar, and restaurant, which serves local dishes such as guinea fowl and pigeon. ◈ *Map C3 • 3 miles (5 km) from Jibacoa off road to Salto Jimenoa • Open for lunch & dinner • $$$*

2 El Jalapeño
Snacks and Mexican food are the fare in this restaurant run by a Puerto Rican family. It has a small disco on the roof. ◈ *Map C3 • Calle Colón, Jarabacoa • Open from midday until late • $$*

3 La Herradura
Good, hearty food from sandwiches to pasta, fish and meat is served in a ranch-style restaurant with rustic decor. Live music at weekends. ◈ *Map C2 • Independencia esquina Duarte, Santiago • Open noon–11pm • $$*

4 Hotel Gran Jimenoa
Overlooking the Jimenoa River, the hotel offers pleasant outdoor seating. The menu features local meats. Dominican families come here for lunch at weekends. ◈ *Map D2 • Av La Confluencia, Los Corralitos • 574 6304 • Open for breakfast, lunch, & dinner*

5 Comedor Gladys
Go for the *menú del día*, served with rice, beans, salad, and any other vegetable in season. ◈ *Map C3 • Luperón 6, Constanza • 539 3626 • Open 7:30–10:30pm Mon–Sat • $*

6 Exquisiteses Dilenia
Local meats such as lamb, rabbit, and guinea fowl are cooked here in various ways. ◈ *Map C3 • Gaston F. Deligne 7, Constanza • 539 2213 • Open 10am–until late • $$*

7 Vista del Yaque
A Parque Recreacional popular day and night hangout with people bathing in the river and patronizing the bar, restaurant, and disco. ◈ *Map C3 • Vista del Yaque, 8 km from Jarabacoa on road to La Ciénaga • Open daily • $*

8 Hotel Alto Cerro
The menu features home-reared geese, guinea fowl, rabbits, and turkeys, and fresh fruits. ◈ *Map C3 • East of Constanza on outskirts of town • 696 0202 • Open for breakfast, lunch, & dinner • $$*

9 Rancho Luna Steak House
This well-known steak house is a treat for meat-lovers. It has an extensive wine list and a piano bar. ◈ *Map C2 • Carretera Luperón 4.5 miles (7.5 km) Santiago • 736 7176 • Open for lunch & dinner • $$$*

10 Kukara Macara
At the foot of the Monumento a los Héroes, this rustic restaurant is decorated in gaucho style. Its fare concentrates on good quality meat, including Angus steaks, as well as tacos, sandwiches, and burgers. ◈ *Map C2 • Av Francia 7 esquina Calle del Sol, Santiago • 241 3143 • Open 11am–3pm • $$$*

Left **Costambar Beach** Right **Paradise Resort, Puerto Plata**

The Amber Coast

THE COSTA DE AMBAR, named after the valuable resin to be found in the mountains inland, is the traditional center of the Dominican tourism industry, rivaled only since the 1990s by the Costa del Coco. Visitors have been coming here since the 1970s, and large purpose-built resorts such as Playa Dorada meet their every need. But there is another dimension to this 200-mile (322-km) vista of sand and mountain, not least in the historical and cultural interest to be found in the 16th-century port city of Puerto Plata, where ancient fortifications and opulent fin de siècle mansions testify to its past. The action-packed beaches of Cabarete and Playa Grande are a magnet for surfers and independent travelers alike. In contrast are the calm and beckoning waters at places such as Sosúa and Playa Dorada.

San Felipe Fortress, Puerto Plata

🔟 Sights

1. Puerto Plata
2. Costambar
3. Cofresí
4. Playa Dorada
5. Sosúa
6. Cabarete
7. Rio San Juan
8. Playa Grande
9. Playa Caletón
10. Laguna Gri Gri

Puerto Plata

1 The biggest town on the North Coast with a long and interesting history, Puerto Plata is sometimes overlooked by visitors in their all-inclusive resorts. This is a shame, because this bustling place has much to offer: not only historic sites but also a range of atmospheric bars and restaurants. The San Felipe Fortress is certainly worth a visit, as is the charming Parque Central, but the highlight is the amazing cable car ride to the top of Pico Isabel de Torres, the lofty mountain that looks over the city and ocean *(see pp16–17)*.

Costambar

2 Only a short taxi ride away from the busy center of Puerto Plata, the beach is just west of town, offering a complete change of atmosphere from the city itself and from the highly developed tourist strip to the east at Playa Dorada. There are no big hotels here, but rather a cluster of tasteful waterfront villas and condominiums, mostly owned by well-heeled locals or foreigners. The beach itself is an extensive strip of soft white sand with calm water and very safe swimming, even if shade is in short supply. The settlement also has a good range of refreshment options. ◈ *Map C1*

Cofresí

3 The advent of the Ocean World theme park in the vicinity of this formerly quiet fishing village, allegedly named after an infamous local pirate, has done much to change its ambience. But the delightfully curved horseshoe cove still draws many visitors to its generous expanse of sand and shade-giving trees. Expensive-looking villas gaze

Playa Dorada

down from the hillsides, while behind the beach stands the up-market Hacienda Resort. The beach becomes much busier at weekends, when the surfing crowd comes in search of its hefty tides, but during the week you're likely to be much more on your own. ◈ *Map C1 • Hacienda Resort: 586 1227*

Playa Dorada

4 The tourist paradise par excellence, this development contains more than a dozen separate resorts, offering every conceivable activity and self-indulgence known to mankind. The range of beach activities encompasses everything from snorkeling to volleyball, while round-the-clock catering provides all sorts of eating and drinking options. The beach itself is a wonderfully white strip of soft sand, cleaned daily, but it can sometimes seem a little crowded, especially in high season. The other most prized asset is the Robert Trent Jones-designed golf course. ◈ *Map C1 • Playa Dorada Golf Course: Open 7:30am–7pm daily; 372 6020; Green fee & hire facilities*

Surfer at Cabarete Beach

5 Sosúa

Like other North Coast communities, Sosúa's transformation from a small fishing town and banana port to a pulsating tourist venue has been little short of astonishing. The place developed a rather unsavory reputation in the 1980s for the worst excesses of tourism, but has been cleaned up since and now offers a great mixture of nightlife and lazy days on the beach. Divided by the beach and bay into two separate and different *barrios*, Sosúa has a distinct tourist area called El Batey, where streets are lined with cafés and stores, and the more authentically Dominican district of Los Charamicos. ◈ *Map D1*

6 Cabarete

The first French Canadian windsurfers arrived in 1984, creating a surfing paradise around the long strip known as Playa Cabarete and a couple of nearby beaches. As a result, a modern tourist town has grown up between beach and lagoon, catering not only to the surfing fraternity but also to a growing range of independent travelers. Surfing, both windsurfing and increasingly kitesurfing, are Cabarete's main *raison d'être*, but there are many other activities on offer. ◈ *Map D1*

7 Río San Juan

A left turn off the coastal Carretera 5 takes you into the small and still unspoilt village of Río San Juan, until recently an isolated rural outpost but now increasingly on the tourist map. There's still a working fisherman's harbor, and the gridiron Barrio Acapulco is filled with boats and other fishing paraphernalia. The village's beach is pretty but very small, so most visitors tend to head farther east down the coast. Rio San Juan's relaxed and friendly atmosphere can be easily sampled in the cafés and restaurants that line the central Calle Duarte. ◈ *Map E1*

8 Playa Grande

A long stretch of perfect golden-hued sand, bordered by forest and demarcated by high cliffs, Playa Grande is unsurprisingly attracting a good deal of tourist development after years of isolation. There are several large-scale all-inclusive resorts, including the Caribbean Village Playa Grande, which boasts a spectacular oceanside 18-hole golf course. The sea is more suitable for surfing than swimming, but at weekends the beach becomes very busy, especially at the end nearer Río San Juan, where food and drink are on sale. This spectacular beach is open to all. *Map E1*

Jewish Exiles

In the 1930s, several hundred Jewish refugees from Europe settled in Sosúa at the invitation of Trujillo, starting a dairy and smoked-meat industry that is still going strong. Now largely dispersed, the Jewish community's history can be explored in the small museum adjacent to the synagogue in El Batey.

Playa Caletón

9 A perfect cove of white sand with mangrove forest surrounding it, this is one of the most beautiful beaches on the North Coast. Even so, it is still not overcrowded yet, and on a week day visitors are liable to be few and far between. At weekends there are more locals around, and you can buy fried fish on the beach. Protected by two rocky and forest-clad promontories, the small bay, known locally by the diminutive La Playita, has shallow clean water, ideal for children. Map E1

Laguna Gri Gri

10 The exotic, mangrove-lined lagoon comes almost into the center of Río San Juan, and boat trips start from a jetty at the northern end of Calle Duarte. Tours take about two hours and pass through the mysterious lagoon landscape. There are crocodiles in the lagoon and a profusion of birdlife, encouraged by the area's environmentally protected status. The Cueva de las Golondrinas (Swallows' Cave), a subterranean passage formed by an earthquake, is home to countless birds, and there are more caves along the Atlantic shoreline. Map E1
• Gaviota Tours, Cabarete: 571 0337

Boats at Laguna Gri Gri

Exploring Puerto Plata

🕐 Half a day is enough to see the main sights of this historically significant town, though if you wish to visit the **Brugal Rum Factory** *(see p17)* more time will be needed. Start in the morning in the **Parque Central** (also known as Parque Independencia), where you will see the attractive gazebo and fine Art Deco cathedral. It is worth bearing in mind that hiring a guide may produce some interesting information. Take a look at some of the restored 19th-century gingerbread-style houses in the old streets around the square.

🕐 Heading towards the sea, you'll reach the **Malecón** *(see p16)*, the long waterside boulevard. Turn left from here to reach the promontory where the much patched-up but impressive Fortaleza de San Felipe stands guard over the harbor entrance. After inspecting the small museum, walk back to the Malecón, where there are plenty of bars and stalls selling cold drinks and snacks. Alternatively, stroll back to Calle John F Kennedy, near the park, and have a drink at **Sam's Bar & Grill** *(see p90)*.

From here it's a fair way to the cable car installation that takes you to the top of the **Pico Isabel de Torres** *(see p17)*, so it is worth taking a taxi. The 20-minute ascent over dense tropical vegetation and the view from the top are breathtaking. At the peak is a pleasant public garden and a cafeteria, suitable for a light lunch.

Left **Sam's Bar & Grill, Puerto Plata** Right **Aguaceros, Puerto Plata**

🔟 Places to Eat & Drink

1 Sam's Bar & Grill
Sam's specializes in American food, grills, burgers, and desserts. It's a good meeting place too. ✪ Map C1 • José del Carmen Ariza 34, Puerto Plata • 586 7267 • Open for breakfast, lunch, & dinner • $$

2 Aguaceros
A restaurant and bar serving an international menu of steaks, seafood, burgers, and Mexican cuisine. ✪ Map C1 • Malecón edif 32, Puerto Plata • 586 2796 • Open 5pm–until late • $$

3 La Parrillada Steak House
This restaurant is on a busy road, but at night you don't notice that. A variety of meat dishes are on offer in pleasant indoor and outdoor settings. ✪ Map C1 • Av Manolo Tavarez Justo, Puerto Plata • 586 1401 • Open for lunch & dinner • $$$

4 Miro on the Beach
A very romantic place with live music performances in the evenings. ✪ Map D1 • Cabarete Beach • 571 0888 • Open 11am–11pm daily • $$–$$$

5 Morua Mai
Choose from a varied menu encompassing pizza, imported meat, fresh fish, and seafood. ✪ Map D1 • Calle Pedro Clisante, Sosúa • 571 2966 • Open 11am–12pm • $$$$

6 La Roca
A friendly place where you can play billiards, browse the book exchange, and eat delicious shrimp and Mexican dishes. ✪ Map D1 • La Roca, Calle Pedro Clisante, Sosúa • 571 3893 • Open 7am–12pm • $$$

Casa del Pescador, Cabarete

7 Cabarete Blú
This beachside bistro offers elegant dining and good food, including both meat and seafood. ✪ Map D1 • Cabarete Beach • 571 9714 • Open 11am–12pm $$$

8 Comedor Loli
A cheerful place to relish Dominican cuisine, mainly chicken, beef, and fish. Check out the menú del día. ✪ Map D1 • Cabarete, at the turning for Parque Nacional El Chocó • Open for lunch & dinner • $

9 Casa del Pescador
In a lovely position on the beach with waves lapping close by. Fish and seafood are the speciality, and the paella is also delicious. ✪ Map D1 • Cabarete • 571 0760 • Open noon–11pm daily • $$$$

10 Bahía Blanca
The restaurant, decorated in cool green and white, is a truly relaxing place to be. ✪ Map E1 • Bahía Blanca, Calle Gastón F Deligne 5, Río San Juan • 589 2563 • Open for breakfast, lunch, & dinner • $$

José Oshay's Irish Beach Pub, Cabarete

🔟 Nightlife

1 Bambú
A beach bar and a disco, Bambú gets extremely lively after midnight. ◊ *Map D1 • Cabarete • Open 11am–6am*

2 Onno's
A hot nightspot with great music, and dancing that goes on into the early hours. There is a "Foam Party" on Saturday nights. ◊ *Map D1 • Cabarete • 383 1448 • Open 11am–6am*

3 Lax
This bistro and bar is a fun venue for beach parties. The bar has a Chinese-style low table, and guests sit on straw matting laid on the sand *(see p57)*.

4 Crazy Moon
One of the better hotel discos, the music changes from steamy tropical rhythms to hip-hop to techno. There's something for everybody *(see p61)*.

5 Voodoo Lounge
A civilized cocktail bar with a dance floor near the beach. You can enjoy a drink and chat without too much noise both inside and outside. ◊ *Map D1 • Calle Pedro Clisante, Sosúa • 571 3559 • Open 7pm–3am daily*

6 D'Latino's Club
A small disco and bar that charges an entry fee if there's a special event or a visiting DJ is playing. ◊ *Map D1 • Calle Pedro Clisante, Sosúa • Open 10pm–untill late*

7 D'Classico
One of the leading night spots in Sosúa, drawing crowds from all over the North Coast, especially unattached males. DJ Pablo Vivax plays a mix of Latin and international music. At weekends, it's mainly Dominican music *(see p61)*.

8 High Caribbean
This popular disco was renovated in 2004. Unusually, it has small indoor and outdoor swimming pools and a terrace. ◊ *Map D1 • Sosúa • Open 10pm–late*

9 Las Brisas
One of the most sought after night spots, Brisas hosts beach volley ball tournaments on Thursday nights *(see p60)*.

10 José Oshay's Irish Beach Pub
A popular beachfront bar that features live acoustic guitar and drum kit performances by Russell, who has an endless repertoire of songs and will also play requests *(see p58)*.

Las Brisas, Cabarete

➡ Following pages **Apartment house in Puerto Plata**

Left **French clock tower, Monte Cristi** Center **El Morro, Parque Nacional** Right **Playa Ensenata**

The Northwest

LITTLE HAS CHANGED IN THIS *isolated and unexplored area of the country. There are hardly any tourist resorts as yet, and time seems to have stopped still in the sleepy towns and villages that dot the empty landscape. A mix of small farms and bone-dry desert wilderness, the region has little of the lushness to be found elsewhere, suggesting that life here is often hard. Yet, despite the sometimes-forbidding appearance of the terrain, the Northwest has distinct attractions, not least its fascinating ecosystems, best explored in the Parque Nacional Monte Cristi. Its beaches, too, are magnificent, and, because of its out-of-the-way character, less developed than those to the east of Puerto Plata.*

Mangroves, Parque Nacional Monte Cristi

Sights

1. Monte Cristi
2. Parque Nacional Monte Cristi
3. Cayos de los Siete Hermanos
4. Playa Ensenata
5. La Isabela
6. Luperón
7. Puerto Blanco Marina
8. Playa Grande
9. Manzanillo
10. Dajabón

Cactus, Parque Nacional

1 Monte Cristi

Like some cowboy movie set, the main town of the region has a rather melancholic feel, set in the scorchingly hot and flat delta of the Río Yaque del Norte. Monte Cristi was once an important port, exporting tobacco and mahogany. The Victorian buildings situated around the Parque Central give an idea of its golden age, which came to an end when a railway link from Santiago to Puerto Plata supplanted it. The French clock tower and various gingerbread mansions are worth a look, especially the ornate Villa Doña Emilia Jiménez. § Map A1

2 Parque Nacional Monte Cristi

Divided between a series of offshore islands, a mangrove delta, and a large inland expanse of desert badlands, the national park shelters a profusion of wildlife, including crocodiles, turtles, and innumerable bird species. The most accessible and interesting part is the flat-topped mountain of El Morro, the imposing outcrop that looks like a sleeping camel. You can walk up some steps from the national park office through a cleavage in the mountain, reaching an isolated beach below, from where it's a relatively short swim to Isla Cabrita. The sea around Monte Cristi is said to be full of shipwrecks (see p40).

3 Cayos de los Siete Hermanos

The "Seven Brothers" are a cluster of tiny islets or cays, flat and dry, lying within the Parque Nacional Monte Cristi. Almost entirely devoid of vegetation, these arid sand spits are surrounded by some of the most pristine reefs in the Caribbean, rarely visited by divers. The islands are a haven for seabirds and turtles, which have always used them as egg-laying territory, but it is reported that poaching is now a major problem. Excursions by boat to the cays can be organized, either from a hotel or from the beach of Playa Juan de Bolaños. § Map A1

4 Playa Ensenata

This stretch of fine white sand shares a headland with the Punta Rucia Beach (see p19) to the west, accessible with some difficulty from the small village of Estero Hondo. Given the remoteness of the place, it's surprising how busy it can become, especially at weekends, when locals come to picnic, swim, and enjoy. It is possibly one of the best beaches in the country with clear shallow water, dramatic mountain scenery, and a welcome absence of vendors and hustlers. Food and drink are usually available at weekends from a few impromptu beach bars. § Map B1

Isla Cabrita, Monte Cristi

5 La Isabela

The site of Columbus's first permanent settlement in the Americas is full of historic interest and natural beauty. Looking out over the Atlantic Ocean, the bluff where the explorer established a European toehold contains the foundations of a warehouse, chapel, and rudimentary hospital. The Parque Nacional La Isabela museum explains the site's significance, while the cemetery nearby is an atmospheric patch of tombstones and acacia trees *(see pp18–19)*. ✎ *Map B1 • Parque Nacional La Isabela: open 9am–5:30pm daily except Sun • Adm*

6 Luperón

Named after a Puerto Plata tobacco magnate, military leader, and president, this small town is typical of the Northwest. It offers little in the way of conventional tourist attractions, but boasts rural atmosphere. The Parque Central is the focal point, with most of the local fish restaurants and bars. Luperón's main claim to fame, however, is its natural bay, which is a favorite with the yachting fraternity. The all-inclusive Luperón Beach Resort is the town's premier hotel. ✎ *Map C1*

7 Puerto Blanco Marina

This magnet for yachties, 2 miles (3.2 km) out of Luperón village, draws a good number of

Puerto Blanco Marina, Luperón

visitors. The marina is located in the estuary, framed by mangrove forests and sheltering hills, with boats moored in the calm anchorage. The bar and restaurant are normally busy, and non-sailors are always welcome. From here it's easy to take a catamaran tour of the estuary and the coast with Rancho Veragua, and to hire diving and snorkeling equipment. With its cosmopolitan crowd of sailing aficionados, the marina has a different feel to the rest of the region. ✎ *Map C1 • Rancho Veragua: 571 8052 • www.ranchoveragua.com*

8 Playa Grande

Not to be confused with the magnificent beach of the same name near Río San Juan, this more modest stretch of sand is Luperón's local seaside

Parque Nacional La Isabela

Dominican Freedom Fighter

One house on Monte Cristi's main square with special historic significance is that formerly owned by Máximo Gómez, the Dominican-born fighter for Cuban independence. Now a museum, it was here that he signed the famous independence declaration along with José Martí before setting off to fight the Spanish colonialists in Cuba.

For reservations at Luperón Beach Resort, Carretera La Isabela call 571 8303

Manzanillo

attraction, backed by a hotel complex. The sea here is inviting, the row of palm trees provides welcome shade, and the sand is pleasantly soft and clean. Nearby are a handful of bars and eating places. ◈ Map C1

9 Manzanillo

The border town and port of Manzanillo, also known since the 1930s as Pepillo Salcedo, is as isolated a spot as you're likely to find in the Dominican Republic. But it's interesting because of its proximity to Haiti and its history as a major banana-exporting center and dock. Nowadays, the port looks very run-down, but there are plans afoot to erect a new industrial complex. From the town itself, you can look over the Massacre River into Haitian territory, but there's no official crossing point here. The nearby lagoon and salt marsh shelters hosts of flamingos and other waders. ◈ Map A1

10 Dajabón

One of three official crossing points with neighboring Haiti, the town's famous for its Monday and Friday markets. Crowds of Haitian vendors cross the bridge over the dividing river and set up stalls near the crossing. The resulting hubbub of commercial transactions is loud and colorful, as Haitians and Dominicans haggle furiously over basics. The market's over by mid-afternoon, so it's worth arriving early to see the action and maybe snap up a bargain or two. ◈ Map A2

From Puerto Plata to La Isabela & Back

Morning

🕐 Leave **Puerto Plata** *(see pp16–17)* early, heading south towards **Santiago** *(see pp14–15)* on the Carretera 5. After about 6 miles (10 km) take a right turn onto a road signposted Maimón and Guzmancito. This rough but passable route takes you through some beautiful rural scenery, including **Maimón Beach** and a series of tiny fishing and farming villages. Keep your eyes firmly on the road, as there are many animals.

🚰 The road comes out at **La Sabana**. A right from here leads to **Luperón**. You can stop here for a drink, or pass through town and stop by **Puerto Blanco Marina** for refreshments.

Another 8 miles (13 km) or so along the Carretera de las Américas through dry woodland and flocks of goats, brings you to the pretty seaside village of **El Castillo**. Just before the village entrance is the turn-off for the **Parque Nacional La Isabela**. An hour or so is sufficient time to look around.

🍴 At lunchtime, go into **El Castillo** and on the right you'll see the **Rancho del Sol** hotel, whose restaurant is recommended for seafood. Or head back to
🍴 the marina or **Luperón's Playa Grande** for food.

Afternoon

Returning to **Puerto Plata**, it's quicker, if less scenic, to go straight into the major junction of **Imbert**, where the Texaco garage marks the road back.

Around the Dominican Republic – The Northwest

Left **Mangroves, Parque Nacional Monte Cristi** Right **Orchids**

🔟 Wildlife

1 Mangroves
The gnarled thickets of vegetation, their roots emerging from mudflats, estuaries, and lagoons, are a unique ecosystem, providing food and shelter to a huge spectrum of birds, fish, and crustaceans.

2 Crocodiles
Like their relatives in Lago Enriquillo *(see pp26–27)*, the Northwest's American crocodiles are not remotely aggressive, fleeing approaching humans and thriving on fish. Their preferred habitat are mangrove forests.

3 Turtles
The offshore cays are favored breeding grounds for the giant leatherback, loggerhead, and small green turtles. They lay large quantities of eggs on the beaches of these desert islands.

4 Pelicans
The huge, heavy brown pelican, with long bill and pouch, can be seen either swimming in the sea or diving spectacularly at a steep angle in search of a fish.

5 Ibises
The gregarious ibises, white with a trademark red bill and face, roost and feed in large flocks. They prefer mudflats and shallow lagoons, where they love to feed on crabs and small fish.

6 Oystercatchers
The American oystercatcher is difficult to confuse with any of the other waders due to its large size, striking black and white plumage, and bright orange bill.

7 Egrets
Taller and whiter than the cattle egret, the snowy egret is another mangrove-loving bird. It nests in colonies in the protective thickets and stalks its prey in the shallow waters *(see p67)*.

8 Orchids
Hundreds of species of orchid of every color abound in the swamps of the Parque Nacional Monte Cristi *(see pp40 & 95)*. Some grow out of trees, the others mysteriously thrive on dry rock faces *(see p64)*.

9 Cacti
The region's desert conditions are ideal for many different sorts of cactus. The best-loved, though, is called *tuna*, the prickly pear, which boasts lovely white flowers and bears edible fruit.

10 Mosquitoes
Obviously, the least-loved of natural inhabitants, these irritating creatures proliferate in the swampy conditions. They can create a genuine health hazard, and cases of dengue fever and malaria have been reported near Haiti.

Ibis

Price Categories

For a three-course meal	
and a beer for one	**$** under $10
including tax and	**$$** $10–$20
service.	**$$$** $20–$30
	$$$$ $30–$40
	$$$$$ over $40

Left **Puerto Blanco Marina, Luperón** Right **Seafood platter**

Places to Eat & Drink

1 Chris & Mady's
This thatched restaurant and bar overlooking the sea is within walking distance of the all-inclusive resorts. ◎ *Map C1 • Cofresí • 970 7530 • Open noon–11pm • $$*

2 Ovando
A fine Mediterranean restaurant with colonial decor. The French chef prepares gourmet meals and delicious desserts. There's an extensive wine cellar, too. ◎ *Map C1 • Sun Village Beach Resort, Cofresí • 970 3364 • Open only for dinner • $$$$*

3 Paul's Pub & Cybercafé
This joint, open until midnight, serves steak, seafood, and curries. The bar's at your service till late too, with German beer on draught. There's live music at times. ◎ *Map C1 • Cofresí • 970 7936 • Open 7am–8pm • $$*

4 Puerto Blanco Marina
Dine in the pretty setting of a lagoon surrounded by mangroves. Enjoy seafood at the restaurant and live music at the popular bar. ◎ *Map C1 • Luperón • 299 4096 • Open for lunch & dinner • Happy hours 5–9pm • $$*

5 Dally
This bistro is quite famous for its fresh and delicious seafood. There is a disco, The Moon, at the rear, and rooms are available for the night. ◎ *Map C1 • 27 de Febrero 46, Luperón • 571 8034 • Open 8am–11pm • $*

6 La Yola
This German-owned eatery near the marina has tasty seafood as well as international cuisine. ◎ *Map C1 • 27 de Febrero, Luperón • Open for lunch & dinner • $*

7 Don Gaspar
A hotel, restaurant, and disco, Don Gasper specializes in Dominican and Spanish dishes. Try the eggs and *mangú*, mashed plantain with onions. ◎ *Map A1 • Pte Jiménez 21 esquina Rodríguez Camargo, Monte Cristi • 579 2477 • Open for breakfast, lunch, & dinner • $$*

8 El Bistro
A charming restaurant set in a colonial courtyard. Its elegant bar and extensive menu of seafood, salads, and pasta make it very popular. ◎ *Map A1 • San Fernando 26, Monte Cristi • 579 2091 • Open 10am–12pm • $$*

9 Comedor Adela
A busy family-run *comedor*, well known for its excellent home cooking. Goat meat is the local delicacy, so don't miss their spicy and highly-satisfying goat stew. ◎ *Map A1 • Juan de la Cruz Alvarez 41, Monte Cristi • 579 2254 • Open for lunch & dinner • $*

10 Cocomar
The food at this eatery is reasonable, although the paella or the seafood platter may cost a little more. ◎ *Map A1 • Monte Cristi • 579 3354 • Open 8am–10pm • $*

Samaná Bay footbridge & sailboats

The Samaná Peninsula

JUTTING OUT INTO THE ATLANTIC OCEAN, *the Samaná Peninsula is a strip of mountainous and verdant land, where the sea is never far away. Water is omnipresent, with views of the sea at every turn, but also in the form of fresh-water streams and cascading waterfalls. Combined with above-average rainfall, this environment produces a spectacle of densely wooded hillsides and coconut groves. Perhaps due to the late arrival of a non-intensive form of tourism, it is more relaxed than elsewhere. History, too, seems to have given it a separate identity. There are stronger traces of a Taino heritage in these parts, and in and around Samaná town are the descendants of English-speaking African-Americans who moved here in the 1820s.*

Left **Samaná harbor** Right **Tropical Lodge sign, Malecón**

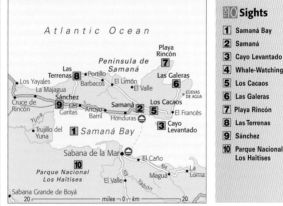

Sights

1. Samaná Bay
2. Samaná
3. Cayo Levantado
4. Whale-Watching
5. Los Cacaos
6. Las Galeras
7. Playa Rincón
8. Las Terrenas
9. Sánchez
10. Parque Nacional Los Haïtises

1 Samaná Bay

The vast, glittering expanse of Samaná Bay comes into view as you drive along the Peninsula's southern coast road. This magnificent natural harbor, sheltered by surrounding hills, forms a perfect haven from hurricanes. In the 19th and early 20th centuries, several European powers as well as the US saw the Bay's potential as a naval base. Luckily, the plans never materialized, and the bay remains largely unspoilt, with beautiful beaches, seaside villages, and fantastic views across the placid water. The bay attracts not just sailors and devotees of water sports, but also humpback whales, which mate and raise their young here. ✆ Map F3

2 Samaná

Santa Bárbara de Samaná is the main town on the Peninsula, a busy little port overlooking the huge bay. While much less of an obvious tourist destination than Las Terrenas (see pp20-21), it has plenty of charm, despite the fact that most of its Victorian-era architecture was demolished in an ill-advised 1970s modernization scheme. The mostly concrete buildings are laid out in a grid system. The focal point is the wide seaside Malecón (boulevard) – a magnet for those who enjoy a walk, especially in the evening. Look out, too, for La Churcha (see p49). ✆ Map F2

3 Cayo Levantado

A stunningly pretty desert island, Cayo Levantado lies a couple of miles offshore from Samaná and is easily reached by regular boat services from

Malecón, Samaná

the Malecón. Such is the tropical charm of this Robinson Crusoe-style cay that it's said that the world-famous Bacardi commercial, featuring white sands and a particularly pretty palm tree, was filmed here. Nowadays, it's advisable to arrive early or visit later in the day, as the island can be very crowded with excursionists around lunchtime. The beaches to the island's south are slightly less busy, but you are unlikely to escape fellow sightseers altogether. ✆ Map F3

4 Whale-Watching

The whale-watching season around Samaná generally lasts from January to March, when an estimated 12,000 humpback whales – the whole population of the North Atlantic – converge on the waters around the Peninsula. The mating and rearing activity takes place in Banca de Plata (Silver Bank) to the north of the Peninsula, and in and around the bay itself, where the shallow and warm water is conducive to courtship displays as well as birthing. Humpback whales can weigh up to 40 tons, so their acrobatics of diving, rolling, and leaping clean out of the water are spectacular.

Malecón, Samaná

Ferries operate daily from Malecón to the island of Cayo Levantado at $20 each way

Playa Bonita, Las Terrenas

Los Cacaos

5 The road eastwards out of Samaná runs along the shoreline, passing numerous beaches. At the small village of Los Cacaos you'll discover a truly wonderful hotel, the Gran Bahía (see p133). Los Cacaos village itself is a modest fishing community, with no tourist facilities. But a rough track up into the mountains leads to an impressive waterfall, with plentiful cold water rushing down the green hillside. Map F2

Las Galeras

6 Lying at the eastern extreme of the Samaná Peninsula, the charming village of Las Galeras has witnessed significant tourist development over the last two decades. But it has not yet lost the ambience of a remote and relaxed fishing community. The main attraction is the beach, a strip of fine sand set in a pretty curving bay backed by cliffs and forested hillsides. Unspoiled by commercial sprawl and hustling, this is a beautiful place, with its calm, shallow, and inviting water. A smattering of hotels, guesthouses, and restaurants offers a choice of accommodation and eating options. Map F2

Playa Rincón

7 Only a robust four-wheel-drive vehicle or a 20-minute boat ride from Las Galeras will get you to the splendidly isolated and spectacular Playa Rincón, hidden by the steep bluffs at each end of the beach. Aficionados claim that this is the best beach on the Peninsula, and it's easy to see why. A 2-mile (3.2-km) stretch of bleached sand is bordered by azure sea and leads back inland to an expanse of coconut trees. While hardly a secret, sheer inaccessibility means that this piece of paradise will stay uncrowded for some time to come (see p44).

Las Terrenas

8 The most developed tourist spot on the Peninsula is a fairly relaxed place, where life revolves around a couple of beaches, seafood restaurants and a busy nightlife. Hotels and guesthouses are mostly small, and situated along the main town beach or the next-door Playa Bonita. A single main street is lined with stores, cafés, restaurants, and nearly all entertainment needs are catered to in town (see pp20–21).

Sánchez

9 Traditionally the gateway to the Samaná Peninsula, bustling Sánchez is where all vehicles

Peninsula for Sale

The strategic significance of the Peninsula and Bay did not go unnoticed by various Dominican presidents in the 19th century, who tried to cash in on this asset. In 1868, President Cabral, for instance, offered the whole Peninsula to the US for a $1-million down payment and an annual rent of $300,000.

For further information on hotels along Los Cacaos, log on to www.occidental-hotels.com

turn off to cross the mountains over to Las Terrenas. It was an important place when a rail connection linked the port to the agricultural powerhouse of the Cibao Valley. But those days are long gone, and now the town is quietly going to seed, kept alive only by its fishing industry and the tourists. The old, prosperous times are visible in a handful of ornate but crumbling gingerbread-style mansions near the waterfront. ◈ Map F2

10 Parque Nacional Los Haïtises

Sánchez is probably the most convenient starting point for a day trip to this wild and isolated nature reserve. A boat departs daily, crossing to the Sabana de la Mar fishing port, where hired guides can lead a boat trip to the small part of the park that's open to visitors. Here, you're confronted by one of the country's most unique landscapes: hump-shaped hillocks rising out of the water and covered with dense tropical vegetation. These strange *mogotes*, along with mangroves and rainforest, shelter a variety of flora and fauna. ◈ Map E3

Old Victorian house, Sánchez

From Samaná to Las Galeras

Morning

🕐 Leave **Samaná** after breakfast, heading eastwards along the Carretera 5. On the left are steep hillsides dotted with small farms and rural settlements, on the right the broad vista over the **Samaná Bay**.

Following **Playa Las Flechas**, a beach named after the arrows that local Taino tribesmen reportedly shot at Christopher Columbus on his first visit, is a small jetty and fishing village called **Simi Baez**. Here you can either take a ferry to the nearby **Cayo Levantado**, or spend some time on the beach or another nearby stretch of sand called **Anacaona**.

The road continues along the coast, revealing exuberant vegetation and idyllic bays, until at **Los Cacaos** you come across the Victorian elegance of the **Gran Bahía** resort, surrounded by colorful gardens. From here, turning northwards, the road passes through an unusual landscape of limestone caves, known as the **Cuevas de Agua**, where locals will be happy to show the subterranean **Taino sites** (see pp32–33).

Afternoon

Aim to arrive in **Las Galeras** in time for lunch. Try the food at **El Marinique** (see p104), which specializes in steaks and seafood, or at one of the other eateries around. Then it's time to visit the beach itself, choosing a shady spot – but not one directly under a cluster of coconuts.

Left **Tropical Lodge, Samaná** Right **Shrimp and broccoli dish**

Places to Eat & Drink

1 L'Hacienda
Eat indoors, or on the pavement outside for fine views of the harbor. This grill and bar serves excellent steaks. ◈ *Map F2 • Malecón, Samaná • 538 2383 • Open from 12am, closed Wed • $$$*

2 Tropical Lodge
This seaside hotel run by Philippe and Brigitte has a good restaurant and the best pizzas in Samaná. ◈ *Map F2 • Malecón, Samaná • 538 2480 • Open for breakfast, lunch, & dinner • $$*

3 Chez Denise
Colorful decor and friendly service makes this a popular stop for snacks as well as meals. Don't miss the delicious crêpes with a variety of fillings, the tasty shrimps, or the salads. ◈ *Map F2 • Calle Principal, Las Galeras • 538 0219 • Open 9am–10pm daily • $$$*

4 El Pescador
A Spanish-owned restaurant with terra-cotta walls and colored lights outside. Seafood is the specialty, with fish, lobster, shrimp, and crab served with a small salad and rice. ◈ *Map F2 • Calle Principal, Las Galeras • 538 0052 • Open 4pm–until late daily • $$$*

5 Villa Serena
Gourmet dining and delightful views of the hotel garden's abundant flowers and palm trees. Open for breakfast, lunch, and dinner *(see p133)*.

6 El Marinique
An open-air seaside restaurant serving terrific food – notably papaya crêpes with maple syrup, and mouthwatering pizza. ◈ *Map F2 • Las Galeras • 538 0262 • Open for breakfast, lunch, & dinner • $$$*

7 Casa Boga
Located in Pueblo de los Pescadores on the beach, with the best fish and seafood in town. Everything's fresh and cooked Basque style *(see p57)*. ◈ *Map F2 • Las Terrenas • 240 6321 • Open 7pm–11pm daily • $$$$*

8 La Capannina
On the beach road heading to El Portillo, this Italian seafront restaurant has an elegant but casual atmosphere. The pizzas are especially fine. ◈ *Map F2 • Las Terrenas • 886 2122 • Open noon–2pm, 7–11pm daily • $$$*

9 Veggies
One of the few vegetarian restaurants in the country, with recipes from Mexico, India, the Arab world, and the Far East. Pretty decor with Afro-Taíno designs, and multi-level seating. ◈ *Map F2 • Calle El Portillo, Las Terrenas • 240 6131 • Open daily • $$*

10 El Paraíso
A beach bar offering refreshing drinks, delectable fish, and shrimp – baked or fried. ◈ *Map F2 • El Paraíso, Playa El Valle • 801 2246 • Open 8am–6pm daily • $*

Price Categories

For a three-course meal and a beer for one including tax and service.

$	under $10
$$	$10–$20
$$$	$20–$30
$$$$	$30–$40
$$$$$	over $40

Le Café de Paris, Samaná

🔟 Clubs & Bars

1 El Mosquito
Set in the Pueblo de los Pescadores, this is a pleasant seafront bar and a popular meeting place. Owners Vero and Alex are expert at blending amazing, large drinks. ✆ *Map F2 • Las Terrenas • 867 4684 • Open 6pm–2am*

2 Syroz
This lovely spot on the beach is run by French proprietor Michelle. There ia an impressive bar, and a dance floor, right on the pristine sand. At weekends there's live jazz and on week days the DJ plays house and soul until dawn *(see p58)*.

3 Nuevo Mundo
The only disco in town, popular with the Dominicans because of its merengue and Latin music. But watch out for the prices, as tourists usually end up paying more. ✆ *Map F2 • Av Duarte, Las Terrenas • Open 9pm–3am*

4 Tropic Banana
The hotel bar is decorated in tropical style, and there's a variety of music including live shows. Tapas is a perfect choice with your cocktails. Golf and petanque are also available. ✆ *Map F2 • Las Terrenas • 240 6110 • $$$*

5 Barrio Latino
Primarily a restaurant, Barrio Latino is also a swinging bar that stays open until midnight. ✆ *Map F2 • Paseo de la Costanera, Las Terrenas • 240 6367*

6 La Yuca Caliente
A Spanish restaurant on the beach under the shade of palm trees. A wonderful setting to enjoy the tapas bar or sample the extensive wine list. ✆ *Map F2 • Libertad 6, Las Terrenas • 240 6634*

7 Indiana Café
This beachside bar and café-style restaurant at the Pueblo de los Pescadores is a perfect night spot. Jazz, reggae as well as house music are usually played on weekends. ✆ *Map F2 • Las Terrenas • 240 5558*

8 Bar Le France
A café-style restaurant and bar on the seafront road, it serves excellent shrimp along with drinks, in the open as well as indoors. Open late, until the last customer leaves. ✆ *Map F2 • Malecón, Samaná • 538 2257*

9 Malecón, Samána
During weekends and fiestas this waterside boulevard springs into action at night, when bars and stalls serving beer and rum appear along its length. ✆ *Map F2 • Samaná*

🔟 Le Café de Paris
Good for light snacks as well as alcoholic beverges. A pleasant location, ideal for watching the boats in the harbor, sipping a cocktail, and listening to loud rock music. ✆ *Map F2 • Malecón, Samaná • 538 2488 • Open until 11pm daily • $*

Following pages **Children playing in Barahona Beach**

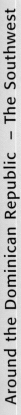

Left **Hotel Las Salinas, Las Salinas** Right **Azua**

The Southwest

A LARGE SWATHE OF TERRITORY EXTENDS *down from the western outskirts of Santo Domingo to the Haitian border, incorporating some of the country's most diverse and dramatic landscapes. The coastline contains a variety of beaches, ranging from remote and undeveloped coves to crowded weekend favorites. Inland, lush, irrigated farmland stands in stark contrast to some of the country's driest desert terrain. Historic towns and cities dot this corner of the Dominican Republic, but its real appeal lies in its natural grandeur. The Sierra de Baoruco is an almost untouched wilderness of mountain rainforest; the Lago Enriquillo, famous for its crocodiles, is better known, but is isolated enough to inspire awe. Tourism has yet to change the character of this region, where the proximity of Haiti is keenly felt, but it's only a matter of time.*

Sights
1 San Cristóbal
2 Baní
3 Las Salinas
4 Azua
5 Barahona
6 Lago Enriquillo
7 Laguna Rincón
8 Sierra de Baoruco
9 Pedernales
10 Parque Nacional Jaragua

Salt pans, Las Salinas

The cathedral, San Cristóbal

1 San Cristóbal

Birthplace of the dictator Trujillo *(see p31)*, this busy provincial center received a great deal of public money during his 30-year regime. It resulted in the construction of an impressive cathedral and surrounding public buildings as well as two nearby residences for Trujillo. The cathedral is certainly worth a visit in order to view the dictator's ornate tomb, which was never used. More interesting are the caves at El Pomier *(see p32)* and the beaches at Palenque and Najayo, to the south of San Cristóbal. ◈ *Map D4*

2 Baní

Set among flat sugarcane-producing land, Baní is an industrious place, its relative wealth due to nearby coffee plantations, salt mining, and commerce. It is also renowned nationally for its particularly delicious mangoes, in season from May to July. Its most famous son is Máximo Gómez *(see p96)*, who with José Martí was the foremost champion of Cuban independence. His house, now containing a small museum, can be reached on foot from the pleasant Parque Central. Also worth a look is Baní's local beach, Los Almendros, with rough sand but with restaurants and plenty of atmosphere at weekends. ◈ *Map D5*

Máximo Gómez, Baní

3 Las Salinas

The small peninsula forming the southern edge of the Bahía de Las Calderas creates an attractive ecosystem, containing salt flats and the most extensive sand dunes in the Caribbean. A naval base is sited here, but visitors can drive through to reach the outpost of Las Salinas, where a hotel and restaurant caters exclusively to windsurfers. The working salt extraction plant is conspicuous through its huge white mountains of finished salt. But the most spectacular views are from the sandy hillsides facing out to the Caribbean. ◈ *Map D5 • Las Salinas High Wind Center: 310 8141*

4 Azua

Swelteringly hot in the plains between sea and mountains, Azua de Compostela looks like an ordinary Dominican town, but it is one of the New World's oldest cities. It was founded in 1504 by Diego de Valásquez, who went on to conquer Cuba. The old colonial settlement was ravaged by war and earthquakes, and the town was rebuilt away from the sea. There are some pretty painted wooden houses at a distance from the main road, but most visitors prefer to head for the Playa Monte Río, a quiet and undeveloped beach with fabulous views over the Bahía de Ocoa and surrounding mountains. ◈ *Map C4*

5 Barahona

The biggest town in the region, the port of Barahona is the gateway to the South-west's natural attractions. A broad seaside boulevard runs the length of the town,

Children at Barahona Beach

and the narrow streets around the Parque Central have some nice old buildings. The advent of an international airport in the 1990s encouraged some tourist development, including a beach-side resort in the town itself. But few visitors confine themselves to Barahona, preferring to explore the coastline to the south and the two nearby national parks. ◈ Map B5

6 Lago Enriquillo

Probably the country's most intriguing natural phenomenon, this huge saltwater lake is eerily atmospheric in its spectacular natural setting. The lake also forms an inland ecosystem, with its mixture of saline water, ancient fossils, and varied wildlife. Chief among these are the American crocodiles that inhabit its main island, the Isla Cabritos (see pp26–27).

7 Laguna Rincón

Filled with fresh rather than salt water, Laguna Rincón, near the village of Cabral, is another surprisingly large lake, the

Boat trip to Isla Cabritos

country's second biggest after Laguna Limón. You can get close to the water on the small road from Cabral which skirts the lake, but the best way is to take a guided boat trip (see p26). The lagoon and surrounding land forms an officially protected Reserva Científica (Scientific Reserve) and is home to a colony of freshwater slider turtles, found only on the Hispaniola Island. ◈ Map B5

8 Sierra de Baoruco

A wild and rugged range of mountains that march west-wards over the Haitian border, these impressive peaks make up the Dominican Republic's second highest sierra. It was in this impenetrable tangle of moun-tains, valleys, and forests that the Taino leader Enriquillo (see p31) assembled his rebel forces and held out for 14 years against the Spanish. Now designated a national park, the range is covered in dense pine forests and subtropical rainforest. There are few passable roads, but it's theoretically possible, with a sturdy jeep, to drive along the rough track from Pedernales to Aguacate. ◈ Map A5

> **Bateyes**
>
> The area around Barahona is dotted with so-called *bateyes*, barrack-like villages usually inhabited by Haitian cane-cutters, who work seasonally on the plantations, and their families. These ramshackle settlements have been condemned over the years as squalid, but for many Haitians and Haitian-descended Dominicans they represent a real sense of community.

9 Pedernales

Pedernales is quite literally the end of the track, the final Dominican outpost before crossing over into Haiti. This remote settlement of one-story concrete buildings huddled together, is hardly a conventional tourist destination. But the place is not without interest, especially on Mondays and Fridays when the no-man's-land between the two countries is the scene of a large open-air market. The village's beach is also worth a visit, and from here it's usually easy to walk over the border. ✎ Map A5

10 Parque Nacional Jaragua

The park comprises the most southerly tip of the country, the Pedernales Peninsula, as well as Isla Beata, an uninhabited scrub-covered island. Covering more than 500 sq miles (1,293 sq km), this is the biggest of the national parks, comprising dry limestone studded with cacti and other desert vegetation. This terrain is home to a huge array of land and sea birds, iguanas, lizards, and bats. The best way to get a sense of its natural importance is to contact the national park office at the village of Oviedo, for the boat tours of Laguna Oviedo. ✎ Map A6 • Open 9am–5pm daily • Adm

Fishermen holding starfish, Pedernales

Day Trip to Lago Enriquillo

Morning

🕐 Set off early from **Barahona**, taking the paved route via Vicente Noble, Tamayo and Galván to the village of **La Descubierta** *(see p27)*. The road passes Haitian *bateyes* and dusty villages, and provides stunning views of the **Sierra de Neiba**. Aim to arrive at the **Parque Nacional de Isla Cabritos**, the lake's official access point just outside La Descubierta, as early as possible and enquire if a boat will leave soon.

The boat trip takes half an hour each way, and you can wander around the rocky island looking for the tame iguanas, or wait for the return trip, which normally involves crocodile-spotting. A welcome cold drink is normally available back at the park office.

Energy permitting, head back to **Postrer Río** and look for signs to **Las Caritas** *(see p27)*, a cave filled with Taino carvings that can be reached by a strenuous 10-minute climb. You could even try the natural swimming pool at La Descubierta, a cold sulfur spring. There are some rudimentary eating places here, but it makes sense to bring along some food and drink, especially water.

Afternoon

Return to Barahona around the lake's loop road, passing the border town of **Jimaní** *(see p27)*, **Duvergé**, and **Cabral**, getting a good view of the freshwater **Laguna Rincón** to your left.

At Parque Nacional de Isla Cabritos, it may be worth waiting to see if anyone else wants a boat trip in order to share the cost

111

Playa Cabo Rojo

Best of the Rest

1 Playa Najayo
A favorite beach with residents of Santo Domingo and San Cristóbal, this strip of golden sand isn't quiet, but it's a good place for a drink and a meal. ✪ Map E5

2 Playa Palenque
Another popular hangout for locals, and rather noisy, the beach does have a quieter end towards the headland and lighthouse, where the sand's slightly darker and the sea rougher. ✪ Map D5

Bahía de las Aguilas

3 Playa Quemaito
One of the first beaches on the long and scenic road south of Barahona (see p110), this is a lovely and little-known stretch of wild coastline, backed by rugged cliffs and woods. ✪ Map B5

4 Larimar Mines
A rough track leads inland from the village of El Arroyo to the open-cast mines where semi-precious larimar is excavated. You can buy pieces of the blue mineral. ✪ Map D5

5 Baoruco
The charming fishing village, now the venue for an all-inclusive hotel, is situated close to a wonderful white-sand beach (see p45), behind which steep wooded hillsides tumble down towards the sea.

6 El Paraíso
The small seaside town called Paradise is aptly named, with a gorgeous, if somewhat unkempt beach. It's shaded by sea grape trees (see p64) and bisected by a cool freshwater stream. ✪ Map B5

7 Polo Magnético
Up in the hills from Cabral is a scientific enigma – a stretch of road that appears to run upwards, but in fact descends. Take off your handbrake and see. ✪ Map B5

8 Cabo Rojo
A desolate expanse of gray sand and rocky bluffs, this empty beach (see p45) shows the scars of bauxite extraction. But it's a wildlife paradise for pelicans and other seabirds.

9 Bahía de las Aguilas
Few visitors make it to this deserted spot, a sweeping bay surrounded by rocky and prickly terrain. It's named after eagles, but there're more gulls, waders, and pelicans on display. ✪ Map A6

10 El Aguacate
As remote a place as you're likely to find, up a tortuous mountain road from Pedernales (see p111). The tiny border post of El Aguacate (Avocado) is almost lost among pine forests and clouds. ✪ Map A5

Left & Right **Brisas del Caribe, Barahona**

Price Categories

For a three-course meal and a beer for one including tax and service.

$	under $10
$$	$10–$20
$$$	$20–$30
$$$$	$30–$40
$$$$$	over $40

🔟 Restaurants

1 Fela's Place
The menu is limited to simple food such as chicken. Fela's is essentially a fast-food restaurant. ◈ *Map D4 • General Leger 55, San Cristóbal • 288 2124 • Open 8am–12pm • $*

2 El Gran Segovia
An air-conditioned restaurant with rustic wooden seating and nautical decor. The cuisine is typically Dominican with lots of local seafood. ◈ *Map C4 • Av Francisco del Rosario Sánchez 31, Azua • 521 3726 • Open for breakfast, lunch, & dinner • $*

3 Cira
The tables at this friendly place with a family ambience, are set in the garden amid trees and flowers. The menu's based mostly around goat and fish. ◈ *Map C4 • Av Francisco del Rosario Sánchez 101, Azua • 521 3740 • Open 9am–11pm daily • $*

4 Francia
Large helpings of good value, traditional Dominican dishes, served in simple surroundings. ◈ *Map C4 • Av Francisco del Rosario Sánchez 104, Azua • 521 2900 • Open 8am–10pm daily • $*

5 Las Salinas
Casual bar and restaurant overlooking Las Salinas *(see p109)*. Popular with sailors for its seafood, burgers, and pasta. ◈ *Map D5 • Puerto Hermoso 7, Baní • 248 0308 • Open 7am–11pm daily • $$*

6 El Gran Artesa
Located in Hotel Caribani, this upmarket, air-conditioned restaurant serves Dominican and international food, either à la carte or from a buffet. ◈ *Map D5 • Sánchez 12, Baní • 522 3871 • Open for breakfast, lunch, & dinner till 12pm • $$*

7 El Quemaíto
A quiet, nicely presented, rustic restaurant with lovely views across a garden and the sea. Both Swiss and local fare are served. ◈ *Map B5 • Juan Esteban, 10km on the road from Barahona to Paraíso • 223 0999 • Open for breakfast, dinner, & lunch • Reservation only • $$*

8 Brisas del Caribe
The best restaurant in town, with delicious seafood and good service, in pleasant surroundings. Packed at lunchtime. ◈ *Map B5 • Brisas del Caribe, Malecón, Barahona • 524 2794 • Open till 11pm • $$*

9 Punta Inglesa
Large Dominican restaurant at Hotel Caribe on the Malecón. Enjoy the air-conditioning indoors or the cool terrace. Good value *menú del día* with seafood. ◈ *Map B5 • Av Enriquillo 21, Barahona • 524 4111 • Open all day • $*

10 Casa Bonita
Eat al fresco in a lovely setting on a hillside. The restaurant is open all day and is very busy during Dominican holidays *(see p132)*.

➤ Following pages **Women at an art stall, Sosúa Beach**

STREETSMART

DOMINICAN REPUBLIC'S TOP 10

Left **Cable car, Pico Isabel de Torres** Right **Sosúa Beach**

🔟 Planning Your Trip

1 Seasons
The country's main tourist season usually runs from December through April, when fares and accommodation are at their dearest. This period is rather drier and less warm than the rest of the year, but temperatures still average 77°F (25°C). The hurricane season lasts from June to November, with most storms occurring from August onwards, but the weather can still be fair.

2 Passports & Visas
All visitors must have a valid passport as well as a tourist card, which can be purchased at the airport on arrival. Visitors must also be in possession of an outward ticket. A departure tax of $10 is payable on leaving the country. It's worth photocopying passport details in case of theft or loss.

3 Currency
The Dominican currency is the peso (RD$), divided into 100 centavos. Dollars are widely accepted, except in more remote rural locations, as are credit cards. Sterling and Euros, on the other hand, are less easy to change.

4 Customs Regulations
Visitors are allowed to bring in 200 duty-free cigarettes and 2 liters of spirits. Customs searches tend to be relaxed, but the Dominican authorities take an extremely hard line on anything connected with firearms or illegal drugs. Food products, especially meat or dairy produce, are confiscated.

5 Insurance
Medical insurance is a must, as any illness or accident will involve paying for treatment and medication, and the best private facilities can be expensive. It is also worth having insurance cover against loss or theft of valuables. Visitors intending to engage in particular sporting activities such as scuba diving or whitewater rafting should ensure that they are covered.

6 Packing
Don't forget the essentials for a beach holiday, as swimwear can be expensive if bought locally. Visitors should also take a few formal jackets for dining out or nightlife, and it's certainly a good idea to have long trousers and long-sleeved shirts for mosquito-infested areas. Those intending to visit the "Dominican Alps" should remember that it can be chilly at night.

7 Health Precautions
There are no particular inoculation requirements for those entering the country, but travelers are advised to ensure that they are protected against tetanus, polio, and Hepatitis A and B. Malaria and dengue fever are mostly a risk in the remote border areas near Haiti. Do not forget to bring prescription drugs.

8 Insect Repellent
This is one of the most vital things to bring with you. It should be applied liberally on exposed skin, especially ankles, and particularly at nightfall. Avoiding mosquito bites is an essential part of staying healthy in the Dominican Republic.

9 Electricity
The country's erratic electricity supply works on a 110-volt system, as in the US and Canada. Plugs are the two-pin North American type, so visitors from Europe may require suitable adaptors. While most Dominicans endure lengthy daily power cuts, due to a creaking power network, nearly all tourist facilities enjoy the benefits of private generators or inverters.

10 Independent Travel
Although some travelers would prefer to be independent and avoid all-inclusive packages, it is worth remembering that pre-booked package deals are almost always better value than last-minute arrangements.

Cruise ship, Santo Domingo

⁨⁨TOP⁩⁨10⁩⁩ Arriving

1 International Airports

Your point of arrival is normally determined by where you are staying, whether in Santo Domingo or one of the principal tourist regions. These have their own international airports. Most scheduled flights land at Las Américas, near Santo Domingo.

2 Tourist Cards

All tourists must present a tourist card at passport control. The card costs $10 and is valid for 90 days. Cards are available at all airports and must be filled in before attempting to pass through immigration.

3 Changing Money at the Airport

It is unlikely that you will arrive already in possession of Dominican pesos, so the airport is a good place to exchange currency. The Banco de Reservas offers a money-changing service at Las Américas in Santiago and Puerto Plata (sometimes closed at weekends). There are also ATMs at all the airports, although these maybe empty during high season.

4 Touts

Incoming flights are often met by hordes of touts, offering a variety of services such as hire cars, money exchange, and guided tours. It is always sensible to decline their offers politely. Visitors arriving on prebooked holiday packages are met by *bone fide* representatives.

5 From Las Américas into Santo Domingo

The Aeropuerto Internacional de las Américas is about 8 miles (13 km) east of the city center. Although there are regular bus services, the best bet is to take a taxi into town. Choose an official taxi driver (look for a brown certificate on the windscreen) and agree the price (about $20) before setting off.

6 Punta Cana Airport

Most of the Punta Cana-Bávaro hotel complexes are within 30 minutes of Punta Cana International, a rather picturesque cluster of thatch-roofed buildings. Hotels usually organize air-conditioned buses to pick up guests, however, taxis are always available, costing about $15 to most hotels.

7 Puerto Plata Airport

Situated between Puerto Plata and Sosúa, the Aeropuerto Internacional Gregorio Luperón is the main entrance point for North Coast visitors. A 15-minute drive into Puerto Plata, or any of the Playa Dorada hotels should cost aound $10.

8 Other Airports

There are also airports at Santiago (Cibao International), La Romana (used mostly to the Casa de Campo resort), Samaná (Arroyo Barril), Las Terrenas (El Portillo), Barahona (María Montéz), and Santo Domingo (Herrera).

9 Arriving by Boat

Several cruise lines include the Dominican Republic on their itineraries, stopping at the new port facilities at Santo Domingo, or close to Casa de Campo.

10 Ports of Entry

Official ports of entry for independent sailors are Santo Domingo, Puerto Plata, Luperón, Samaná, and Punta Cana. A customs fee of $10 is applicable per person, payable at the customs and immigration facility, granting 30 days immigration clearance.

Directory

Airports
- Aeropuerto Internacional de las Américas: 549 1069
- Punta Cana International: 686 2312
- Aeropuerto Internacional Gregorio Luperón: 586 1992
- Cibao International: 233 8000 • Arroyo Barril: 248 2566 • María Montéz: 524 4144
- Herrera: 547 3454

See p127 *for more information on tour operators*

Left **Bus station, Santo Domingo** Right **Taxi, Santo Domingo**

📖10 Getting Around

1 Internal Flights

Air Santo Domingo offers regular and reliable connections between Santo Domingo, Puerto Plata, Punta Cana, and Samaná, as well as a service to San Juan, Puerto Rico. Caribair flies between the capital and Port-au-Prince, Haiti, stopping at Barahona. Internal flights are much more expensive than the alternatives but useful if you're in a hurry.

2 Long-Distance Buses

Very good value and surprisingly comfortable bus connections are provided by several companies and cover the entire country. Metro is good for North Coast destinations, while Caribe Tours has a comprehensive network of buses west and north of the capital. Nearly all buses are air conditioned, with toilets and good seats. A great way to explore the Dominican Republic.

3 Taxis

There's no shortage of taxis, especially in tourist areas. Your hotel will be able to recommend a reputable local firm or call a taxi on your behalf, but it is always sensible to agree the price before setting off as most are unmetered. Many drivers are friendly and knowledgeable, and can be hired as a taxi-guide for an excursion.

4 Públicos & Guaguas

Públicos are private cars that act as shared taxis, plying fixed routes and normally crammed with passengers. *Guaguas*, on the other hand are mini-vans that start from a local bus station and are ideal for short trips without luggage.

5 Motoconchos

The ultimate low-budget option, the *moto-concho (see p123)* is a small motorbike, where the passenger sits on the pillion. Quite speedy but also dangerous.

6 Car Rental

Car rental is widely available but quite expensive, so do book ahead with one of the more established international companies such as Hertz or Avis. Local operators Nelly are good.

7 Motorcycles

You can easily hire a motorcycle at any of the main tourist areas, normally a small but still quite powerful Honda or Suzuki. Expect to pay $20-$30 per day.

8 Bicycles

Bicycles can be rented from specialist firms such as Iguana Mama *(see p127)* or from some of the beach resorts. Helmets should always be worn, and caution taken on main roads and in urban areas.

9 Ferries from Samaná

The only regular ferry service in the country, Samana Net, links the port of Samaná with Sabana de la Mar across the Bay of Samaná, but vehicles cannot be transported at present. It's a pleasant trip across the scenic water and a good way of avoiding an otherwise long drive around the Bay, but you'll have to use public transport at the other side.

10 On Foot

Apart from hiking in the Cordillera Central, walking isn't much practiced by visitors, though it's a practical way of exploring city centers such as Santo Domingo's Zona Colonial, the heart of Puerto Plata, or Santiago. Don't forget to bring comfortable shoes.

Directory

Internal Flights
• Air Santo Domingo: www.airsantodomingo.com • Caribair: www.caribair.com

Buses
• Metro: 556 7126
• Caribe Tours: www.caribetours.com.do

Car Rental
• Hertz: www.hertz.com • Avis: www.avis.com

Ferries
• Samana Net: www.samana.net

Left **Central La Romana** Right **A traffic light**

📖10 Driving Tips

1 Drive on the Right
If you're planning to rent a car, remember that driving can be challenging as well as exciting. In theory, Dominicans drive on the right, but overtaking vehicles often occupy the middle of the road, even on blind corners.

2 Animals
Animals, especially goats, present a threat in some of the Dominican Republic's more remote rural areas, as they tend to wander unchecked on to the road. This is a particular problem after nightfall when visibility is already limited. Dogs are also frequent victims of collisions.

3 After Dark
Driving after dusk is generally a risky business, as potholes, animals, and other obstacles are less clearly visible. Main thoroughfares are generally safer than isolated country roads, but bear in mind that some drivers have vehicles without working headlights and that others don't dip their headlights, causing dazzling among oncoming drivers. It's generally safer, except in well-lit urban streets, to stop driving before nightfall.

4 Speed Bumps
Most towns and villages have an array of speed bumps on their outskirts, sometimes accompanied by a police or military checkpoint. These are meant to enforce the country's speed limits of 48 miles per hr (80 km/hr) on main roads and 25 miles per hr (40 km/hr) in towns.

5 Checkpoints
Particularly common in the regions closest to the Haitian border, these generally involve little more than slowing down and a nod or wave from a bored soldier. Occasionally, military personnel decide on a cursory inspection of a vehicle, but don't be alarmed.

6 Police
The Dominican police used to enjoy a certain notoriety for demanding bribes from motorists, often on the spurious pretext that a speed limit had been broken. This is much less common now, after a campaign by the authorities, but isolated cases do still occur. You can either hand the policeman a small note (RD$20 or RD$50) or simply insist that you do not speak Spanish until he gives up.

7 Tolls
The big *autopistas* out of Santo Domingo (towards Las Américas airport, Santiago, San Cristóbal, and Haina) have automatic toll booths on exits from the capital. You will require the exact small change to pass through (currently RD$5 per vehicle), payable also on returning.

8 Fuel
Gas is relatively expensive, due to rising world prices and a weak Dominican peso. Petrol stations (known as *bombas*) are plentiful in the main towns but sometimes extremely rare in remote country areas. It is worth filling up whenever possible. You should also remember that many *bombas* close at about 8pm.

9 Flat Tires
Punctures are a constant problem on the country's poorly maintained road network and when driving on rough tracks. It can be extremely expensive to buy new tires, and a much cheaper option is to use the services of one of the legions of tire repair men (*gomeros*), whose workshops are to be found in every town.

10 Traffic Lights
Most Dominican towns are built on a classic grid system, with alternating up and down streets and traffic lights at intersections. With the chronic problem of power supply, however, traffic lights often don't work, so it is advisable to approach each junction on the assumption that any other car will fail to give way.

Left **Thesaurus bookshop** Right **White-water rafting, Jarabacoa**

🔟 Sources of Information

1 Tourist Offices Abroad
Official Dominican tourist offices in the United States, Canada, and the United Kingdom provide brochures and routine information on major destinations. For more details on specific activities, smaller hotels, and independent travel you may be better off consulting independent agencies, tourist offices, and websites.

2 Local Tourist Offices
There are tourist offices scattered throughout the country, with the main offices situated in Santo Domingo, but few have the resources or expertise to answer more than the most basic questions. A better bet would be one of the many specialist tour operators *(see p127)*.

3 Websites
There is a huge amount of information about the country available on the Internet. Search engines are a useful means of locating specific information.

4 English-Language News
There is currently no English-language newspaper published in the Dominican Republic, but an invaluable source of news and general information is available on the website DR1, which has a daily news service as well as lots of material on travel and tourism.

5 Spanish-Language Press
There is a lively local press, with several daily and evening titles published in Santo Domingo. Some are available online, such as *Listín Diario* and *Diario Libre*.

6 Local Travel Agencies
Dotted around the country, these are often a reliable source of information on specific regions and activities.

7 Maps
There are several good maps of the country, the best published by Berndtson & Berndtson. In Santo Domingo, the best outlet for maps is Mapas Gaar.

8 Bookstores
Several bookstores in Santo Domingo have a good range of maps, guidebooks, and other travel-related literature.

9 Guides
Although some individuals offering their services as guides can be a nuisance, there are many well-qualified and informed guides. It is worth asking at your hotel or among any local contacts for a recommended and reliable person, who may also be a taxi driver *(see p118)*.

10 Adventure Trips
For sports and activity holidays it is worth consulting Dominican Adventures' website *www.drpure.com* for maps, information, and a great many useful links.

Directory

Tourist Offices Abroad
• US: 1 (212) 588 1012
• Canada: 1 (514) 499 1918 • UK: 0207 405 4202

Local Tourist Offices
• *Santo Domingo: Palacio Bonde* • *Puerto Plata: Malecón 25*
• *Santiago: Duarte & Estero Hondo*
• *Samaná: Carretera Las Terrenas*

Websites
• *www. debbiesdominicantravel. com* • *www. hispaniola.com* • *www. dominican-rep.com*
• *www. dominicanrepinfo.com*
• *www.dr1.com*

News Sources
• *Listín Diario: www. listin.com.do* • *Diario Libre: www.diariolibre. com.do*

Map & Book Stores
• *Mapas Gaar: Arzobispo Nouel 355, Santo Domingo*
• *Thesaurus, Av Lincoln, Santo Domingo*
• *Librería La Trinitaria, Arzobispo Nouel 160, Santo Domingo*

For more information on the Dominican tourist offices log onto www.dominicanrepublic.com

Left **Public phones, Santo Domingo** Right **Internet café, North Coast**

Banking & Communications

1 The Peso
The Dominican peso is divided into 100 centavos, with notes of 5, 10, 20, 50, 100, 500, 1,000, and 2,000. The last two are often impossible to change, especially in rural areas. The only coin in everyday use is the 1 peso. The peso's exchange rate against the US dollar and other currencies fluctuates widely, and there is an official rate announced daily in newspapers.

2 Using US Dollars
In tourist areas and all-inclusive hotels, prices are often quoted in US dollars, which are preferred to pesos. In more remote places, however, the peso is still the preferred currency.

3 Banks & ATMs
There are many foreign-owned and local banks, all of which will change dollars at the official rate, though queuing at the counter can be a lengthy business. Opening hours are normally 8:30am to 5pm, Monday to Friday. Major banks such as the Banco Popular, Banco Leaon, and Banco del Progreso operate ATMs, which accept the cards such as MasterCard and Visa.

4 Bureaux de Change
Casas de cambio offer more or less the same rates as banks and will cash traveler's checks. They also have longer opening hours than banks.

5 Credit Cards
The major cards are widely accepted in hotels, restaurants, and tourist-oriented stores, but not in out-of-the-way places or corner stores. Look at the slip carefully before signing and make sure that you are not charged in US dollars if you think you are paying in pesos. Credit cards can also be used for cash advances at certain banks, but this will involve at least 5 percent commission.

6 Telephones
Public phones are plentiful and normally reliable, operated by several private companies. It's a good idea to buy a phone card (Verizon) for between RD$25 and RD$500 (see p124), which allows you to make cheap international calls. Calls made from hotels are often quite expensive, so call family collect.

7 Phone Codes
Calls made within the Dominican Republic require a 7-digit number with no area code. To call outside the country, first dial 00 followed by the country code. To call the Dominican Republic from abroad, dial the international access number (00 in the United Kingdom, 011 in the United States and Canada) then 809 and the 7-digit number.

8 Charges
Phone charges can vary enormously, from exorbitant hotel rates to much cheaper calls made from a phone center, where the operator dials for you and you sit in a booth. Calls between different towns and districts are charged at the same rate as those to the US. It is much cheaper in all cases to call before 8am, after midnight, or on Sundays.

9 Mail
Mail is dreadfully slow, and you should not use street mail boxes. Special delivery (entrega especial) services are available at big post offices, but even these are unreliable. It is better to use an international courier company if sending anything important or valuable.

10 Internet
Internet services have expanded and improved dramatically but are still often victims of power cuts and technical problems. The main tourist areas now have a plethora of Internet cafés, but not all have quick DSL connections, and you are normally charged by the hour. Despite all the problems, email is still the best way of keeping in touch.

Left **Police car, Santo Domingo** Center **Pharmacy, La Descubierta** Right **Bottled water**

Security & Health

Emergencies
1 The police, fire services, and public ambulance system can be contacted by phone by dialing 911. Generally, the police are responsive to any reports of crime against tourists, although reporting a theft may involve a lengthy bureaucratic procedure. Help is usually available from your relevant embassy or consulate. A private ambulance company, Movimed, can be reached on 535 1080.

Health Services
2 Public hospitals and clinics are, to say the least, rudimentary. Your hotel will normally be able to recommend a doctor, probably US-trained and English-speaking. In the event of a serious emergency, you should contact your insurance company.

Pharmacies
3 There are pharmacies in all the major towns, mostly well stocked, and you do not necessarily require a prescription to obtain medicines. Check that the medicines you are given are not generic and cheaper versions, and that they are not past their sell-by date.

Personal Safety
4 Violent crime against foreigners is rare, but in tourist areas there is a risk of pick-pocketing and bag-snatching. Avoid dark and lonely spots, do not carry large amounts of cash, or flaunt expensive watches or cameras, and keep your valuables in the hotel, preferably in a safe.

Harassment
5 Most visitors experience some level of harassment, especially in well-trodden tourist areas, from individuals offering a range of services. Rudeness rarely produces a satisfactory outcome and may be counter-productive.

Police Stations
6 Every town and village has its local police station, but few low-ranking officers will speak English. If you are the victim of theft, your hotel or embassy should be able to help you.

Consulates
7 The US, Canada, and UK all have embassies with consular services in Santo Domingo.

Women Travelers
8 Foreign women can receive a fair amount of unwanted attention from Dominican men, but this mostly takes the form of harmless verbal intrusions. The most effective response is a stony glare or cold indifference.

Food Hygiene
9 The best way to avoid an upset stomach is to steer clear of certain foods, notably meat, fish, and dairy products that have been allowed to stand too long on a buffet counter.

Water
10 Do not drink the tap water. Some people prefer to not even brush their teeth with it, and you should make sure that ice cubes are made from purified water. Bottled water is cheap and widely available.

Directory

Medical Clinics
• Clínica Abreu: Beller 42, Santo Domingo, 688 4411 • UCE University Hospital: Av. Máximo Gómez, Santo Domingo, 221 0171
• Centro Médico Punta Cana: El Salado, Bávaro, 552 1506
• Hospiten Bavaro: Higüey, 686 1414
• Hospiten Santo Domingo: 381 1070
• www.mdtravelhealth. com

Police Stations
• Av. Independencia, Santo Domingo, 533 4046 • Carretera 5, Puerto Plata, 586 2331
• Calle del Sol, Santiago, 582 2331

Embassies & Consulates
• US: Santo Domingo, 221 2171 • Canada: Santo Domingo, 689 0002 • UK: Santo Domingo, 540 3132

Left **Taxi, Santo Domingo** Right **Motoconchos, Las Terrenas**

TOP 10 Things to Avoid

1 Money-Changing Scams
Never accept the tempting offer of a better exchange rate from any would-be money-changer who approaches you. Although less of a problem than previously, the informal money-changing system almost invariably involves a hefty rip-off, where you discover that you have a lot fewer pesos than apparently counted out.

2 Taxi Scams
Most taxis are unmetered, and although there are set prices for regular journeys, they are not widely visible. Most taxi drivers are honest, but a minority will attempt to bamboozle visitors out of large sums. Always agree a price before setting off.

3 Traffic Jams
Roads in and around Santo Domingo can be appallingly congested, especially at weekends and public holidays (see pp50–51), when a large number of the capital's inhabitants head for the beaches or mountains. You should try to avoid traveling at peak periods, notably Friday afternoons and evenings, and Sunday evenings. Congestion is particularly heavy when re-entering the capital Santo Domingo and attempting to cross the Ozama River into the city center.

4 Running Low on Gas
It makes sense to fill up whenever possible, particularly if you are driving in the Cordillera Central or the remote Northwest, as running out of fuel (see p119) can be time-consuming and highly expensive.

5 Running out of Cash
Banks (see p121) in the main towns are also often closed at weekends, although casas de cambio (bureaux de change) are more flexible in their opening times. When heading off into the country, make sure to withdraw enough cash to cover any eventuality.

6 Drugs
Though the Dominican Republic has less of a drugs culture than other Caribbean nations, there are still drug dealers in tourist resorts, offering cocaine, marijuana, and ecstasy at some nightclubs and other venues. The Dominican police take a very harsh view of all drug use and Dominican prisons are extremely unpleasant places.

7 Sunstroke
It is easy, especially with children, to underestimate the power of the tropical sun, and sunburn and sunstroke are the most common threats to an enjoyable stay. Visitors should avoid the hottest part of the day, between noon and 3pm and cover themselves with a strong sunscreen, even when the weather seems predominantly cloudy. Drink plenty of water to avoid dehydration.

8 Mosquitoes
The bane of many visitors, these annoying and potentially harmful insects are found in most parts of the country, especially near stagnant water and mangroves. Wear as much repellant (see p116) as possible and make sure that your room is fitted with a proper screen.

9 Sand Fleas
Although not particularly dangerous as such, the sand flea's bite is surprisingly painful. These creatures seem most active on beaches at dusk, but appear to be repelled by suntan lotion or baby oil. When bitten, hydrocortisone cream helps in reducing pain and itching.

10 Motoconchos
Motorbikes are the cheapest method of public transport (see p118). They are also physically dangerous not only for the unhelmeted passengers, but also for pedestrians, who are often involved in accidents with these vehicles. Look both ways before crossing the road.

Left **Sam's Bar & Grill, Puerto Plata** Right **Tourists lounging at a bar, Playa Sosúa**

Budget Tips

1 Go Low-Season
You can save a good deal, both booking package deals and as an independent traveler, by visiting during the low season, between September and the middle of November. This is the end of the hurricane season, though this should not deter tourists.

2 Look for Budget Deals
Many travel agents offer substantial last-minute discounts, but this means that you will have to leave at short notice. It's also worth noting that prebooking all-inclusive deals is inevitably much cheaper than flying independently and then trying to book a room.

3 Look for Hotel Offers
If you are traveling independently, it is worth trying to negotiate cheaper rates at hotels, either by opting for a room-only arrangement or by haggling politely. Some Dominican hotels, especially in Santo Domingo and Santiago, will offer cheaper rates at weekends when commercial travelers are not using their rooms.

4 Public Transport
Buses and *guaguas* are a fraction of the price of hiring a car or taking a taxi and are a good way of seeing the countryside and meeting some local people. Though not luxurious, *guaguas* are regular and reliable and will get you from your hotel into town or to the beach for a few pesos.

5 Street Food
Cheap food on sale at street stands or in family-run *comedores* may present something of a health risk. But if you make sure that it is freshly cooked, a plate of chicken with rice and beans will cost little more than $2. The principal rule is to have the food in question cooked in front of you and to avoid salads and fruit that may have been washed in tap water.

6 Happy Hours
Many hotels, bars, and restaurants operate an early evening happy hour, when drinks are half price or sometimes accompanied by complimentary snacks. The best time to look for two-for-one deals is between 6pm and 8pm, especially in the tourist areas.

7 Share a Guide
It can cut the cost of a guided tour or hiring a taxi driver/guide for a day by sharing with other visitors, as the guide will normally charge a fixed fee, irrespective of whether there is one or four clients. Taxis can also normally be shared between up to four people during trips.

8 Haggling
Most local stallholders and shopkeepers not unreasonably assume that a tourist can afford to pay above the going rate for a T-shirt, necklace, or souvenir. Haggling is fine in places other than conventional supermarkets, and if you are persistent and polite, you may succeed in knocking down the price enough for you to feel you've got a bargain and the vendor to make a profit.

9 Avoid Tourist Stores
Shops and stores in tourist-oriented malls and hotels are often overpriced. You're much better off buying items such as soap or shampoo, liquor and snacks, from the local neighborhood *colmado*. Likewise, clothing and souvenirs are a good deal cheaper in open-air or covered markets, or in the informal beach markets in coastal resorts.

10 Buy a Phone Card
Making phone calls from hotel rooms can be very expensive. It is also not always convenient to have handfuls of one-peso coins to make calls from public phones. The best, and most economical, solution is to buy a phone card (see p121) which can be used with any phone, including the one in your room.

Left **Presidente Beer** Center **Brugal Rum Factory, Puerto Plata** Right **Hemingway's Café**

⌐10 Eating & Drinking Tips

1 Restaurants, Cafeterías, & Comedores

Eating places in the Dominican Republic range from formal and swanky restaurants, where a meal can easily cost $50 per head, to humble *cafeterías*, where the price is more likely to be under $5. *Cafeterías* tend to offer a choice of precooked meals. On the other hand, *comedores*, or small local restaurants normally offer a single lunchtime dish.

2 Snacks & Fast Food

There are plenty of burger and chicken outlets in the main towns and tourist resorts, but more interesting are the Dominican versions of fast food available at snack stands. Cooked on demand and with high turnover, these tasty snacks are probably less risky than lukewarm buffet meals.

3 Breakfasts

Dominicans like a good filling breakfast, and most hotels will offer at least some local favorites such as *mangú*. There will always be a choice of tropical fruits, various breads and pastries and, of course, Dominican coffee.

4 Buffets

Buffets are the easiest way of feeding crowds of people at the same time in a large hotel. But they can be somewhat bland and boring, especially after a few days. The other problem is that food left standing around in the heat can quickly attract a host of microbes, and many food poisoning cases have been traced to buffet food.

5 Fried Food

Dominican food, rather like its Spanish equivalent, is often heavy on the oil, with an emphasis on deep frying. Vegetables such as green beans have been known to arrive at table doused in oil. Some of the grease can be avoided by asking for grilled meat or fish known as *a la parrilla* or *a la plancha*.

6 Bills & Tipping

A 12 percent government tax is automatically added to restaurant bills, as is a 10 percent service charge. As it's very unlikely that your waiter or waitress will end up with that money, you should also leave a 10 percent tip, if you think the service merits it.

7 Beers & Wine

Wine is mostly imported from Spain or South America and is relatively expensive. The "house wine" at all-inclusives is often undrinkable. But Dominican beer, most conspicuously available under the Presidente label, is excellent and served ice cold in even the most remote village shop.

8 Rum

Rum is the serious drinker's first choice, and there are three very good brands: Brugal, Barceló, and Bermúdez, which come as dark or lighter varieties. *Añejo (see p55)* means aged, and is usually smoother and more expensive than the standard types. Avoid over-sugary cocktails and try a good rum like a brandy or on the rocks.

9 Bars

Outside tourist areas, where bars *(see pp58–59)* are often run by expats with a strong sense of how to please foreigners, Dominican bars can be rough-and-ready places, dominated by a spirit of machismo and not particularly comfortable for women, even accompanied. You're often better off having a drink in the corner store, which will inevitably have a huge and well-stocked refrigerator. Bars tend to open and close late.

10 Buy a Bottle

On an evening out it's quite customary, if you're in a group, to order a bottle of rum to share. It will come with a bucket of ice, and you can order soft drinks such as Coke as a mixer.

➤ **See also pp56–61** for restaurants, bars and nightlife venues

Left **Hotel Gran Almirante, Santiago** Center **Playa Sosúa** Right **A fruit punch**

Special Needs

1 Senior Travelers

All-inclusive hotels, in particular, have a long experience of meeting special needs in terms of mobility, and most are equipped with elevators and other amenities. In rural areas, however, there are fewer concessions to old age, and public lavatories or restrooms, for instance, are in very short supply.

2 Disabled Travelers

Some progress has been made in recent construction and refurbishment of hotel facilities, especially in the all-inclusive sector, to accommodate the needs of disabled travelers. But with the exception of a few well-trodden tourist sites, the country is not geared up for disabled needs, and there are no specially adapted cars.

3 Children

A few simple precautions such as not drinking tap water and excessive exposure to the sun should prevent avoidable health problems. There are plenty of activities for younger visitors *(see pp36–37)*.

4 Childcare

Most of the big all-inclusives organize supervised children's activities on the beach or around the pool, usually in the form of a club. If you want to go out till late without children, it

may be possible to hire a baby-sitter. Ask at the hotel reception.

5 Diapers

Disposable diapers or nappies are available at the big supermarkets and sometimes, at a high price. Travelers with babies should bring at least an emergency supply of their preferred brand, as those on sale are of inferior quality.

6 Prescription Medicines

People with regular medicine requirements should bring more than what they estimate they will need in case of delay or emergency.

7 Vegetarians

Vegetarianism has yet to catch on in a big way, although there are vegetarian restaurant options in Santo Domingo and the tourist resorts. Non-meat eaters may be forced to make do with fried eggs or omelets as well as filling plantains and rice and beans. In the big hotels the choice is better, as buffets tend to feature a selection of salads and vegetable dishes.

8 Gay & Lesbian Travelers

The Dominican Republic is an overwhelmingly Catholic and macho society, and most people take an unsympathetic view of gay and lesbian

relationships. Therefore, it is not a good idea for non-heterosexual couples to go in for public displays of affection. Gay relations are not actually illegal, but harassment and even violence are not unknown. There is, on the other hand, an openly gay scene in the capital, and gay relationships are much more tolerated in the laid-back resorts of Sosúa, Las Terrenas, and Cabaret.

9 Getting Married

Tying the knot in the Dominican Republic is a relatively straightforward affair, providing you have the appropriate documents, such as birth certificate, passport, and notarized certificate of single status. Although a Dominican wedding requires some forward planning, it is now an increasingly popular option. For more details, log onto Debbie's Page: *www. debbiesdominicantravel. com/wedding*.

10 Getting Divorced

Only one married partner is required to be present at a Dominican "quickie" divorce, although divorce by mutual consent is much more straightforward than a contested divorce. The key to a smooth procedure is to find a reliable local lawyer. For advice, log onto *www.ct-divorce.com/Domin*.

Left **Parque Nacional del Este** Right **Isla Catalina**

TOP 10 Tours & Special Interests

1 Tours of the Zona Colonial
Although the best way to explore Santo Domingo *(see pp8–9)* is on foot, there are several tour operators which offer bus tours. Another favorite is the night tour, which includes a visit to a bar, restaurant, or, quite often, the Guácara Taina nightclub. All tours will feature the services of an English-speaking guide.

2 Tours of the Samaná Peninsula
The natural attractions of the Samaná Peninsula *(see pp100–105)* can be hard to reach if you don't know where you are going. Call on the services of a local operator such as MS Tours.

3 Tours of the North Coast
The beaches to the west of Puerto Plata are not easily accessible, and the trip to the historic site of La Isabela *(see pp18–19)* can be arduous. Operators based in and around Puerto Plata organize tours to a range of North Coast attractions as well as the city of Puerto Plata *(see pp94–99)* itself.

4 Jeep Safaris
Jeep safaris are a great way for travelling through the remoter parts of the Dominican countryside, such as small villages, hard-to-

find waterfalls or swimming spots. Companies such as Bávaro Runners and Turinter organize tours that will pick you up from your hotel in groups.

5 Helicopter Tours
A short 20- or 30-minute helicopter flight over a spectacular stretch of coast or mountain landscape can be an unforgettable experience. Several companies such as El Caballo Tours lay on flights for 2 or 3 passengers per trip.

6 Bird-Watching
The exciting range of the country's birdlife can be appreciated by amateurs or real connoisseurs, either by simply watching colorful birds in the hotel grounds or by seeking out rare species with a specialist operator such as Eagle-Eye Tours.

7 Whale-Watching
The whale-watching season is between January and March and is concentrated around the Samaná Peninsula, where boats can take you out for short or longer expeditions. Caribbean Bikes is one of several companies that organize tours that get you close to the playful whales.

8 Cycling
Cycling is probably the healthiest and most rewarding way to get off the beaten track and see

real rural life. Iguana Mama and Caribbean Bikes are expert in helping cyclists of all ages and abilities.

9 Diving
There are many diving companies dotted around the island, either independent or attached to particular hotels. Dominican Diving Vacations is a good starting-point for exploring.

10 Fishing Trips
Small boats can be hired informally without too much difficulty at places such as Bayahibe or Palmar de Ocoa, but for big game fishing for marlin or bonito you'll need to contact a specialist operator through a website.

Directory

Local Tours
• www.turinter.com
• www.cocotours.com
• www.dominicantravel.com
• www.samana.net

Activity Tours
• www.bavarorunners.com
• www.caribbeanbiketours.com
• www.elcaballotours.com • www.eagle-eye.com • www.iguanamama.com

General Information
• www.dominican-diving.com • www.charternet.com

Barceló Bávaro Beach Resort, Playa Bávaro

Accommodation Tips

1 Tipping
Tipping hotel staff is at your discretion but it's customary. Tip porters US$1 per bag carried to your room. If you leave US$1 a day in your room you'll find your house-keeper is more likely to put fresh flowers or elaborate towel decorations on your bed.

2 Location
Beachfront hotels will cost more than those off the beach and a room with a sea view will be costlier than one over-looking the garden. In Punta Cana nearly all the hotels are all-inclusive and you're not expected to stray far from your hotel, as you're miles from anywhere. To explore the island, a North Coast destination is more convenient, with better public transport.

3 High Season
Prior booking is essential at Easter, when Dominicans take their holidays. In Cabarete there is a second high season, relating to windsurfing conditions, from June 15 to September 15.

4 All-Inclusives
Punta Cana, Bávaro, and Bayahibe in the East and Cofresí, Playa Dorada, and other North Coast beach resorts dominate all-inclusive hotels. Quality and service vary but basically you get what you pay for. Buffet food is monotonous while alcoholic drinks are usually limited to national brands of rum and beer with watered down wine for dinner and extra charges for any-thing else. Check what's on offer, what sports you can opt for and for how long, whether there is an *à la carte* restaurant and how many times you can eat there. Some hotels require you to book your activities and meals days in advance, while others are more flexible.

5 Hotel Tax
All hotels charge an extra 22 percent on top of the room rate. This is made up of 12 percent VAT and 10 percent service and is subject to change according to national taxation legislation. Room rates do not include the tax.

6 Accommodation Types
In Santo Domingo, hotels range from international style modern hotels run by foreign chains to boutique hotels in restored colonial man-sions. There are also a few cheap guesthouses and aparthotels. There are dozens of all-inclusive beach hotels on the North and East Coasts and several medium-sized ones for independ-ent travelers. Up in the mountains there are country inns and guesthouses offering comfortable lodging. Fewer options are available in the West.

7 Visitors with Disabilities
Very few hotels have facilities for the disabled. As there is no Dominican legislation requiring hotels to provide such amenities, it is best to try the international hotels where the parent company upholds the same standards world-wide *(see p126)*.

8 Air Conditioning
Most medium and upper quality hotels have air conditioning and their own generator as back up. Smaller hotels often suffer blackouts. Most places have ceiling or free-standing fans.

9 Language
Staff at hotels in the capital and resorts usu-ally speak English and often one other European language. In out of the way areas it is less common. A few Spanish phrases *(see p142)* will help you on excursions as well as in hotels.

10 Reservations
It is advisable to book at least your first few nights prior to arrival, although it is possible to travel around in low season without pre-booking. It is essential to book well in advance during the high season.

High season is December 15 to April 15, when hotel rates peak.
For more information See p116

Streetsmart

Price Categories

For a standard, double room per night (with breakfast if included), taxes and extra charges.

$	under $30
$$	$30–50
$$$	$50–100
$$$$	$100–150
$$$$$	over $150

Wilson's Beach House, Cabarete Beach

🔟 Budget Hotels

1 Aída, Santo Domingo

A friendly, family-run hotel, set above a music store in the heart of the shopping area of the old city. The rooms are basic but clean and adequate. Those with a balcony have a fan but some rooms have no windows though they have air conditioning. Book in advance as it's usually full. ◈ Map N5 • El Conde 464 & Espaillat • 685 7692 • No smoking • $

2 Independencia, Santo Domingo

An inexpensive hotel with a convenient location near the Parque Independencia. The rooms are clean, with soap and towels provided. Some rooms have no windows. The downside is the noisy bar, open apparently all night. Art exhibitions are sometimes held here and there is a language school across the street. ◈ Map M6 • Estrella y Arzobispo Nouel • 686 1663 • No air conditioning • $

3 Duque de Wellington, Santo Domingo

This hotel lies in the pleasant residential area of Gazcue, just west of the Colonial Zone. It offers budget rooms, each with a fridge and TV. There is also a bar and a restaurant. ◈ Map M3 • Av Independencia 304, Gazcue • 682 4525 • $$

4 Mi Casa, Constanza

In a central location, walking distance from transport, shops, and restaurants. There's also a comedor in the hotel that serves local food. ◈ Map C3 • Luperón y Sánchez • 539 2764 • $

5 Brisas del Yaque, Jarabacoa

This place is excellent value for money. The rooms are small but the furnishings are in good condition. Rooms have a small balcony, a TV, and air conditioning. There is no restaurant but the hotel is within walking distance of all the bars, cafés, and restaurants. ◈ Map C3 • Luperón esquina Peregrina Herrera • 574 4490 • $

6 Colonial, Santo Domingo

The rooms are small but well equipped with air conditioning, good bathrooms with hot water, a fridge, and a TV. The staff is friendly. ◈ Map K2 • Av Salvador Cucurullo 115 • 247 3122 • $

7 Wilson's Beach House, Cabarete

Popular with windsurfers, who can bring and store their gear here. Upstairs, there are four rooms with bathrooms which share a sitting room, fridge, and a large balcony. Downstairs, there is a three-bedroom apartment. Electricity and hot water are solar powered. ◈ Map D1 • Cabarete Beach • 571 0733 • $–$$ • www.wilsonsbeachhouse.com

8 Docia, Samaná

This guesthouse overlooks La Churcha with views of the bay and the dock below. The rooms are simple with private bathrooms and hot water. Each room has a fan. Those upstairs are brighter with large windows to catch the breeze. ◈ Map F2 • 538 2041 • No air conditioning • $

9 Fata Morgana, Samaná

Off the beaten track, this is a quiet, peaceful place popular with backpackers and budget travelers. The rooms sleep up to four people and have bathrooms. You may use the kitchen and barbecue. ◈ Map F2 • Turn off Fabio Abreu near the French school • 836 5541 • No air conditioning • $

10 Hotel Bayahibe, Bayahibe

The hotel lies within walking distance of dive shops and places to eat as well as the beach. Most rooms can sleep four and are equipped with one or two beds, a TV, fridge, kitchenette, air conditioning or fan, and a balcony. There is Internet access in the lobby. ◈ Map G4 • Calle Principal • 833 0159

Cabana Elke, Bayahibe

🔟 Self-Catering Hotels

1 Cayo Arena, Monte Cristi

A small complex of two-bedroom apartments on the seashore. The kitchens and bathrooms are basic but adequate. The complex has a small pool and a bar. ✆ Map A1 • Playa Juan de Bolaños • 579 3145 • $$$

2 Haciendas El Choco, Sosuá

This place has villas with every comfort including private swimming pools, large thatched verandas, and tropical gardens. It offers full service with maid, gardener, and pool maintenance. ✆ Map D1 • Carretera El Choco • 571 2932 • $$$$$ • www.elchoco.com

3 Palm Beach Condos, Cabarete

These roomy condos on the beach are privately owned, individually decorated, and walking distance from the beaches and bars in Cabarete. ✆ Map D1 • 571 0758 • $$$–$$$$ • www. cabaretecondos.com

4 Bahía de Arena, Cabarete

A group of villas and apartments set on the outskirts of Cabarete, within in walking distance of shops and restaurants. There is a central communal area with a pool, a Jacuzzi, a tennis court, and a small shop for essential supplies, as well as a Swiss restaurant. ✆ Map D1 • 571 0370 • $$$–$$$$ • www.cabaretevillas.com

5 Velero Beach Resort, Cabarete

One of the most luxurious hotels in Cabarete, offering flexible accommodation. Rooms and suites can be combined to make apartments, which have good kitchens and large living areas. All have a sea view. Good discounts in low season. ✆ Map D1 • Calle La Punta 1 • 571 9727 • $$$$ • www.velerobeach.com

6 Aparthotel Caracol, Cabarete

A 50-room hotel offering studios and apartments, all equipped with kitchenettes. Excellent for families as it has a playground, ice-cream parlour, and baby-sitting facilities. Also caters to kiteboarders, with a kite school and a free lesson included in the rates. ✆ Map D1 • 571 0680 • $$$ • www.hotelcaracol.com

7 Plaza Lusitana, Samaná

In the center of Las Galeras village, the suites and apartments are built above shops around a courtyard garden. Accommodation is spacious with air conditioning, fans, and tiled floors. Apartments have sofa beds in the living room. Suites are large single rooms with a sitting area, kitchenette, and bathroom. ✆ Map F2 • Plaza Lusitana, Las Galeras • 538 0093 • $$$–$$$$ • www.plazalusitana.com

8 Playa Colibrí, Las Terrenas

One of the larger complexes of studios and apartments with one or two bedrooms, a pool, Jacuzzi, and parking. You may negotiate daily, weekly, or monthly rates. ✆ Map F2 • Francisco Caamaño Deñó • 240 6434 • No air conditioning • $$$ • www.playacolibri.com

9 Bella Vista Condos, Boca Chica

This attractive modern complex of condos offers parking and 24-hour security. Each condo has two bedrooms and bathrooms, and is comfortably furnished with tiled floors, air conditioning, and fans. Monthly rates are a particularly good deal. ✆ Map F4 • 523 6070 • $$$

10 Cabana Elke, Bayahibe

Studio apartments in a small hotel just behind the all-inclusive Wyndham Dominicus Beach Resort (see p133), where you can buy a day pass to use the facilities. They also have a restaurant and a bar. ✆ Map G4 • Playa Dominicus • 689 8249 • $$$ • www.viwi.it

Most hotels now have websites and e-mail addresses for booking on the Internet

Price Categories

For a standard, double room per night (with breakfast if included), taxes and extra charges.

$	under $30
$$	$30–50
$$$	$50–100
$$$$	$100–150
$$$$$	over $150

Sofitel Nicolás de Ovando, Santo Domingo

🔟 Town Center Hotels

1 Sofitel Nicolás de Ovando, Santo Domingo

This restored historic mansion dating from the 16th century features massive stone walls and high ceilings in every elegant room and suite. A pool overlooking the Rio Ozama, a small state-of-the-art gym, and a gourmet restaurant complete the picture. ◎ *Map P5 • Calle Las Damas • 685 9955 • Dis. access • $$$$$ • www.sofitel.com*

2 Sofitel Francés, Santo Domingo

This small hotel set in a renovated colonial mansion with a central courtyard has a gourmet French restaurant. The rooms are elegant and comfortable. Buffet breakfast, tax, and service are included in the rates. ◎ *Map P5 • Las Mercedes esq Arzobispo Meriño • 685 9331 • Dis. access • $$$$$*

3 Courtyard by Marriott, Santo Domingo

The rooms and service here are of an excellent standard and offer great value for money as breakfast is included. Free Internet access is available in the lobby. They also have a gym, self-service laundry, a pool, restaurant, and delivery service from other restaurants. ◎ *Map L3 • Av Máximo Gómez 50-A • 685 1010 • Dis. access • $$$$*

4 Meliá Santo Domingo

An international Sol Meliá chain hotel offering rooms and suites for business and leisure travelers. It also offers good transport links. ◎ *Map M4 • Av George Washington 365, Santo Domingo • 221 6666 • Dis. access • $$$$ • www.solmelia.com*

5 Renaissance Jaragua Hotel & Casino, Santo Domingo

The Jaragua is one of the top business travelers' hotels, with rooms and communications facilities designed to meet modern standards. Leisure activities and nightlife attract Dominicans as well as foreigners. ◎ *Map M4 • Av George Washington 367 • 221 2222 • Dis. access • $$$$ • www.marriott.com*

6 Hostal Nicolás Nader, Santo Domingo

This colonial mansion, dating back to 1502, is now a small, charming inn belonging to the Nader family, who also own several art galleries. The walls are hung with modern art and all the furnishings and decorations are artistic and stylish. Live music can often be heard at weekends. ◎ *Map N5 • Duarte y General Luperón • 687 6674 • $$$$ • www.naderenterprises.com/hostal*

7 Mercure Comercial, Santo Domingo

This 20th-century hotel includes buffet breakfast, tax, and service in the tariff. It's convenient for business travelers as it provides Internet access and phone. ◎ *Map N5 • El Conde esq Hostos • 688 5500 • Dis. access • $$$*

8 El Beaterio, Santo Domingo

A guesthouse in a renovated home featuring a roof terrace and a patio. Airport transfers can be arranged. Breakfast included in the rates. ◎ *Map N6 • Duarte 8 • 687 8657 • $$*

9 Aloha Sol, Santiago de los Caballeros

Rooms and suites are well appointed with air conditioning, TV, good service, and the benefit of a restaurant on site. Breakfast included in the rates. ◎ *Map C2 • Calle del Sol 150 • 583 0090 • Dis. access • $$$*

10 Hodelpa Gran Almirante Hotel & Casino, Santiago de los Caballeros

It's popular with business travelers and rooms have a mini bar and Internet access. There's also a pool and two Spanish restaurants. ◎ *Map C2 • Av Estrella Sadhalá 10, Los Jardines • 580 1992 • Dis. access • $$$ • www.hodelpa.com*

For more information on Courtyard by Marriott or to make online bookings log onto www.marriott.com/SDQCY

Left **Rancho Baiguate, Jarabacoa** Right **Casa Bonita, Barahona**

TOP 10 Rural Hotels

1 Hotel Rancho Constanza & Cabañas de la Montaña, Constanza

Rancho Constanza has a modern Alpine-style block with rooms and basic cabins for families. There is a restaurant, a playground, and volleyball and basketball courts. The staff can arrange mountain sports. 🅂 *Map C3 • Calle San Francisco de Macorís 99, Sector Don Bosco • 539 3268 • No air conditioning • $$$ • www. ranchoconstanza.com*

2 Alto Cerro

Accommodation ranges from camping to spacious self-catering villas, all spread along the hillside. The restaurant serves local meat, fruits, and vegetables. Horseback riding or quad-bike excursions can be arranged. 🅂 *Map C3 • East of Constanza heading to Colonia Kennedy • 539 1429 • No air conditioning • $–$$$*

3 Mi Cabaña, Constanza

This is a complex of small townhouses with kitchenettes, each of which can sleep four guests. Breakfast is provided but there is no restaurant. They also have a pool, a bar, and a volleyball court. 🅂 *Map C3 • Carretera Gen Antonio Duvergé, Colonia Japonesa • 539 2930 • No air conditioning • $–$$$*

4 Rancho Baiguate, Jarabacoa

This place is known for adventure sports such as river rafting, tubing, hiking, and horse riding. The rooms vary in size, standard, and price, with all meals included, but no TV, air conditioning, or other modern conveniences. 🅂 *Map C3 • La Joya • 574 4940 • No air conditioning • $$–$$$ • www.ranchobaiguate.com*

5 Pinar Dorado, Jarabacoa

A single block of hotel rooms set in a pleasant garden surrounded by pine trees with a pool. It's comfortable but not remarkable. Air conditioning and TV in all rooms, buffet breakfast, lunch, and dinner on offer. Meal plans available. 🅂 *Map C3 • Carretera a Constanza 1km • 574 2820 • $$$*

6 Gran Jimenoa, Jarabacoa

Outside town on the edge of the beautiful Río Jimenoa, the rooms here are nothing fancy, but are comfortable, with TV. Rates include breakfast and taxes. 🅂 *Map C3 • Av la Confluencia, Los Corralitos • 574 6304 • $$ • www.granjimenoa.com*

7 California, Jarabacoa

This small, family-run hotel has simple rooms with fans, all on the ground floor, leading out to a central patio and pool. Breakfast is $5, while other meals of *comida criolla* can be arranged on request. Local activities can be arranged. 🅂 *Map C3 • Calle José Durán E 99 • 574 6255 • No air conditioning • $*

8 Blue Moon Retreat, Cabarete

Accommodation is in four bungalows and comprises four individually decorated suites, a family suite, and a two-bedroom apartment with kitchen. Breakfast is included and the restaurant serves Indian food. 🅂 *Map D1 • Los Brazos • 223 0614 • $$–$$$ • www.bluemoonretreat.net*

9 Casa Bonita, Barahona

The rooms in these bungalows come with fans and air conditioning but no TV or phone. The restaurant is good but rather expensive *(see p113)*. 🅂 *Map B5 • Carretera de la Costa km16, • 696 0215 • $$$ • www.casabonitadr.com*

10 Aquarius, Bonao

The rooms and suites offer the latest communications technology and are designed for business travelers as well as vacationers. There is a restaurant, a mini bar, and cocktail lounge. 🅂 *Map H4 • Calle Duarte 104 • 296 2898 • Dis. access • $$–$$$ • www.aquariusbonao.com*

Hotel staff at Aquarius can arrange excursions with boat rides to the Hatillo dam, caves, and rivers as well as horseback riding

Atlantis, Las Terrenas

Price Categories

For a standard, double room per night (with breakfast if included), taxes and extra charges.

$	under $30
$$	$30–50
$$$	$50–100
$$$$	$100–150
$$$$$	over $150

🔟 Beach Hotels

1 Sosúa-by-the-Sea
This pleasant hotel offers the advantages of booking either room-only or all-inclusive. The rooms are clean and tidy, with air conditioning, and there is a pool. Northern Coast Diving is on site for scuba diving lessons and excursions. ✪ *Map D1 • Sosúa • 571 3222 • $$$ • www. sosuabythesea.com*

2 Kitebeach, Cabarete
A kiteboarder's paradise, with accommodation packages including kite lessons, storage, repairs, and cleaning of all gear. You can choose budget or superior rooms, air-conditioned suites, or apartments. Negotiate special rates for long stays. Buffet breakfast is included and Internet access is free. ✪ *Map D1 • 571 0878 • Cash only • $$–$$$ • www. kitebeachhotel.com*

3 Villa Taína, Cabarete
You may sit on the beachside restaurant and watch the windsurfers from the school next door. A short stroll along the sand takes you to various places to eat and drink, and to the nightlife venues of Cabarete. The rooms have air conditioning, and a balcony or terrace. Breakfast is included in the rates. ✪ *Map D1 • Calle Principal • 571 0722 • $$$ • www.villataina.com*

4 Windsurf Resort, Cabarete
An apartment hotel with comfortable bedrooms, kitchenettes, and a pool. Free equipment for guests includes kayaks, sailing boats, and windsurfers. There is an Italian bistro. ✪ *Map D1 • 571 0718 • $$–$$$ • www. windsurfcabarete.com*

5 Bahía Blanca, Río San Juan
This is a wonderful place to admire the changing turquoise hues of the sea, so clear you can see the coral. The rooms are simple and clean with basic amenities. Meal plans are available. ✪ *Map E1 • Gastón F Deligne 5 • 589 2528 • $ • bahia. blanca@verizon.net.do*

6 Villa Serena, Las Galeras
The rooms are impeccably decorated and furnished with ceiling fans and air conditioning, while the restaurant offers gourmet cuisine (see p104). ✪ *Map F2 • 538 0000 • $$$$ • www.villaserena.com*

7 Atlantis, Las Terrenas
This hotel is known for its French food. The rooms are large and comfortable with marble bathrooms, and some have air conditioning. ✪ *Map F2 • Mitterand, Playa Bonita • 240 6111• $$$ • www. atlantisbeachhotel.com*

8 Barceló Bávaro Beach Resort
An all-inclusive resort comprising five hotels, offering a golf course, a 24-hour casino, Internet café, shops, and a convention center. A small tram shuttles guests around the property. ✪ *Map H4 • Playa Bávaro • 686 5797 • Dis. access • $$$$–$$$$$ • www. barcelo.com*

9 Wyndham Dominicus Palace/Beach, Bayahibe
Two all-inclusive hotels for the price of one. The Palace is better and more expensive, but shares the Beach's private beach. There are many restaurants, but you have to reserve two days in advance for the à la carte ones. Also on offer: bars, disco, theater, kids' club, soccer, and organized excursions. ✪ *Map G4 • Playa Dominicus • 687 8583 • Dis. access • $$$$ • www.vivaresorts.com*

10 Gran Bahía, Samaná
An all-inclusive, elegant hotel not normally found in Dominican resorts. The service is good and there are many facilities, including a 9-hole golf course and horse riding. Boat trips and whale-watching excursions can be arranged. ✪ *Map F2 • Carretera a Las Galeras • 538 3111 • Dis. access • $$$$$*

General Index

Acknowledgements

The Author

James Ferguson is a writer and publisher who has specialized in the Caribbean for 20 years. He has written books on Haiti, the Dominican Republic, and Grenada and is a regular contributor to *Caribbean Beat* magazine.

Photographer Jon Spaull

Additional Photography

Deni Bown, Andy Crawford, Eric Crichton, Ken Findlay, Derek Hall, Colin Keates, Richard Leeney, David Murray, Rob Reichenfeld, Tim Ridley, Lucio Rossi, Jules Selmes, Clive Streeter, Debi Treloar, Jerry Young.

Cartography Credits Base mapping for Dominican Republic and Santo Domingo derived from Netmaps www.netmaps.es

AT DK INDIA:

Managing Editor Aruna Ghose
Art Editor Benu Joshi
Project Editor Vandana Bhagra
Editorial Assistance Pamposh Raina
Project Designers Baishakhee Sengupta, Divya Saxena
Senior Cartographer Uma Bhattacharya
Cartographer Alok Pathak
Picture Researcher Taiyaba Khatoon
Fact Checker Griselda Gonzalez Nin
Indexer & Proofreader Bhavna Seth Ranjan
DTP Co-ordinator Shailesh Sharma
DTP Designer Vinod Harish

AT DK LONDON:

Publisher Douglas Amrine
Publishing Manager Vicki Ingle
Managing Art Editor Jane Ewart
Senior Cartographic Editor Casper Morris
Senior DTP Designer Jason Little
DK Picture Library Romaine Werblow, Hayley Smith, Gemma Woodward
Production Shane Higgins

Picture Credits

t-top; tl-top left; tlc-top left center; tc-top center; tr-top right; cla-center left above; ca-center above; cra-center right above; cl-center left; c-center; cr-center right; clb-center left below; cb-center below; crb-center right below; bl-bottom left, b-bottom; bc-bottom center; bcl-bottom center left; br-bottom right; d-detail.

Every effort has been made to trace the copyright holders of images, and we apologize in advance for any unintentional omissions. We would be pleased to insert the appropriate acknow-ledgements in any subsequent edition of this publication.

The publisher would also like to thank the following for their assistance and kind permission to photograph at their establishments:

Acuario Nacional; Adrian Tropical; Aguaceros; Atlantis; Baoruco Beach Resort; Barceló Bávaro Beach Resort; Brisas del Caribe; Brugal Rum Factory; Cabana Elke; Café Cito; Casa Bonita; Casa de Campo; Columbus Aquapark; Crazy Moon;

Hemingway's Café; Hodelpa Gran Almirante Hotel & Casino; Jet Set; José Oshay's Irish Beach Pub; La Casa del Pescador; La Isabela; La Résidence; Las Brisas; Las Salinas; Le Café de Paris; Librería Thesaurus; Mesón de la Cava; Museo de Arte; Museo de Larimar; Museo del Hombre Dominicano; Museo Prehispánico; Museum at the Parque Nacional Histórico La Isabela; On the Waterfront; Paradise Resort; Rancho Baiguate; Sam's Bar & Grill; Sofitel Nicolás de Ovando; Tropical Lodge; Vesuvio; Wilson's Beach House.

The publishers would like to thank the following individuals, companies and picture libraries for their kind permission to reproduce their photographs.

CASA DE CAMPO: 24cla, 25tl, 25tr, 25cr, 25cb.
CORBIS: 31tr; Tony Arruza 7bl, 8-9c, 21cr, 24-25c, 27cra; Tom Bean 37tr, 16-17c, 50c, 50tr, 78-79,100t; Bettmann 30 tr, 31tl; Richard Bickel 12-13c; 110tc, 106-107, Duomo 39tr; Reinhard Eisele 68-69; Macduff Everton 23tl, 38bl; Franz-Marc Frel 6cl, 14-15c, 20-21c; Jeremy Horner 10-11c, 11cr; Patrick Johns 65bl; Danny Lehman 7cl, 22br 51bl, 114-115; Massimo Listri 28-29; Ludovic Maisant 49tr, 53tr; Douglas Peebles 64tl; Giraud Philippe 38tr; Carl & Ann Purcell 92-93; Joel W. Rogers 2tl, 4-5; Kevin Schafer 64c, 64tl; Jim Sugar 18clb; Nevada Wier 111bl.

CLARA GONZALEZ
www.DominicanCooking.com: 63bl

WILSON'S BEACH HOUSE: 129tl.

All other images © Dorling Kindersley
For further information see www.dkimages.com

Dorling Kindersley Special Editions

Dorling Kindersley books can be purchased in bulk quantities at discounted prices for use in promotions or as premiums. We are also able to offer special editions and personalized jackets, corporate imprints, and excerpts from all of our books, tailored specifically to meet your own needs.

To find out more, please contact: (in the United Kingdom) – Sarah.Burgess@dk.com or Special Sales, Dorling Kindersley Limited, 80 Strand, London WC2R 0RL; (in the United States) – Special Markets Department, DK Publishing, Inc., 375 Hudson Street, New York, New York 10014.

Phrase Book

In an Emergency

Help!	¡Socorro!	soh-**koh**-roh
Stop!	¡Pare!	**pah**-reh
Call a doctor!	¡Llame a un médico!	**yah**-meh ah **oon meh**-dee-koh
Call an ambulance!	¡Llame una ambulancia!	**yah**-meh ah **oon**ah ahm-boo-**lahn**-see-ah
Call the fire department!	¡Llame a los bomberos!	**yah**-meh ah lohs bohm-**beh**-rohs
policeman	el policía	ehl poh-lee-**see**-ah

Communication Essentials

Yes	Sí	see
No	No	noh
Please	Por favor	pohr fah-**vohr**
Thank you	Gracias	**grah**-see-ahs
Excuse me	Perdone	pehr-**doh**-neh
Hello	Hola	**oh**-lah
Bye (casual)	Chau	chau
Goodbye	Adiós	ah-dee-**ohs**
What?	¿Qué?	keh
When?	¿Cuándo?	**kwahn**-doh
Why?	¿Por qué?	pohr-**keh**
Where?	¿Dónde?	**dohn**-deh
How are you?	¿Cómo está usted?	**koh**-moh ehs-**tah** oos-**tehd**
Very well, thank you	Muy bien, gracias	mwee bee-**ehn grah**-see-ahs
Pleased to meet you	Mucho gusto	**moo**-choh **goo**-stoh
See you soon	Hasta pronto	ahs-tah **prohn**-toh
I'm sorry	Lo siento	loh see-**ehn**-toh

Useful Phrases

That's fine	Está bien	ehs-**tah** bee-**ehn**
Great/fantastic!	¡Qué bien!	keh bee-**ehn**
Where is/are...?	¿Dónde está/están...?	**dohn**-deh ehs-**tah**/ehs-**tahn**
How far is it to...?	¿Cuántos metros/ kilómetros hay de aquí a...?	**kwahn**-tohs **meh**-trohs/kee-**loh**-meh-trohs **eye** deh ah-**kee** ah
Which way is it to...?	¿Por dónde se va a...?	pohr **dohn**-deh seh **vah** ah
Do you speak English?	¿Habla inglés?	**ah**-blah een-**glehs**
I don't understand	No comprendo	noh kohm-**prehn**-doh
I would like	Quisiera/ Me gustaría	kee-see-**yehr**-ah meh goo-stah-**ree** ah

Useful Words

big	grande	**grahn**-deh
small	pequeño/a	peh-**keh**-nyoh/nyah
hot	caliente	kah-lee-**ehn**-teh
cold	frío/a	**free**-oh/ah
good	bueno/a	**bweh**-noh/nah
bad	malo/a	**mah**-loh/lah
open	abierto/a	ah-bee-**ehr**-toh/tah
closed	cerrado/a	sehr-**rah**-doh/dah
full	lleno/a	**yeh**-noh/nah
empty	vacío/a	**vah**-see-oh/ah
left	izquierda	ees-key-**ehr**-dah
right	derecha	deh-**reh**-chah
(keep) straight ahead	(siga) derecho	(**see**-gah) deh-**reh**-choh
near	cerca	**sehr**-kah
far	lejos	**leh**-hohs
more	más	mahs
less	menos	**meh**-nohs
entrance	entrada	ehn-**trah**-dah
exit	salida	sah-**lee**-dah
elevator	el ascensor	ehl ah-sehn-**sohr**
restrooms	baños/ servicios	**bah**-nyohs/
women's	de damas	deh **dah**-mahs
men's	de caballeros	deh kah-bah-**yeh**-rohs

Post Offices & Banks

Where can I change money?	¿Dónde puedo cambiar dinero?	**dohn**-deh **pweh**-doh kahm-bee-**ahr** dee-**neh**-roh
How much is the postage to...?	¿Cuánto cuesta enviar una carta a...?	**kwahn**-toh **kweh**-stah ehn-vee-**yahr** oo-nah **kahr**-tah ah
I need stamps	Necesito estampillas	neh-seh-**see**-toh ehs-tahm-**pee**-yahs

Shopping

How much does this cost?	¿Cuánto cuesta esto?	**kwahn**-toh **kwehs**-tah **ehs**-toh
I would like...	Me gustaría...	meh goos-tah-**ree**-ah
Do you have?	¿Tienen?	tee-**yeh**-nehn
Do you take credit cards/ traveler's checks?	¿Aceptan tarjetas de crédito/ cheques de viajero?	ah-**sehp**-tahn tahr-**heh**-tahs deh **kreh**-dee-toh/ **cheh**-kehs deh vee-ah-**heh**-roh
I am looking for...	Estoy buscando...	**ehs**-tohy boos-**kahn**-doh
expensive	caro	**kahr**-oh
cheap	barato	bah-**rah**-toh
white	blanco	**blahn**-koh
black	negro	**neh**-groh
red	rojo	**roh**-hoh
yellow	amarillo	ah-mah-**ree**-yoh
green	verde	**vehr**-deh
blue	azul	ah-**sool**

antiques store	la tienda de antigüedades	lah tee-**ehn**-dah deh ahn-tee-gweh-**dah**-dehs
bakery	la panadería	lah pah-nah-deh-**ree**-ah
bank	el banco	ehl **bahn**-koh
bookstore	la librería	lah lee-breh-**ree**-ah
butcher's	la carnicería	lah kahr-nee-seh-**ree**-ah
cake store	la pastelería	lah pahs-teh-leh-**ree**-ah
jeweler's	la joyería	lah hoh-yeh-**ree**-yah
market	el tianguis/ mercado	ehl tee-ahn-goo-ees/mehr-**kah**-doh
newsstand	el kiosko de prensa	ehl kee-**ohs**-koh deh **prehn**-sah
post office	la oficina de correos	lah oh-fee-**see**-nah deh kohr-**reh**-ohs
shoe store	la zapatería	lah sah-pah-teh-**ree**-ah
supermarket	el supermercado	ehl soo-pehr-mehr-**kah**-doh
travel agency	la agencia de viajes	lah ah-**hehn**-see-ah deh vee-**ah**-hehs

Transportation

When does the… leave?	¿A qué hora sale el…?	ah **keh oh**-rah **sah**-leh ehl
Where is bus stop?	¿Dónde está la parada de buses?	**dohn**-deh ehs-the tah lah pah-**rah**-dah deh **boo**-sehs
Is there a bus/ train to…?	¿Hay un camion/ tren a…?	eye oon kah-mee-**ohn**/trehn ah
platform	el andén	ehl ahn-**dehn**
ticket office	la taquilla	lah tah-**kee**-yah
round-trip ticket	un boleto de ida y vuelta	oon boh-**leh**-toh deh **ee**-dah ee voo-**ehl**-tah
one-way ticket	un boleto de ida solamente	oon boh-**leh**-toh deh **ee**-dah soh-lah-**mehn**-teh
airport	el aeropuerto	ehl ah-ehr-oh-poo-

Sightseeing

art gallery	el museo de arte	ehl moo-**seh**-oh deh **ahr**-teh
beach	la playa	lah **plah**-yah
cathedral	la catedral	lah kah-teh-**drahl**
church	la iglesia/ la basílica	lah ee-**gleh**-see-ah/ lah bah-**see**-lee-kah
garden	el jardín	ehl hahr-**deen**
museum	el museo	ehl moo-**seh**-oh
ruins	las ruinas	lahs roo-**ee**-nahs

tourist information office	la oficina de turismo	lah oh-fee-**see**-nah deh too-**rees**-moh
ticket	la entrada	lah ehn-**trah**-dah
guide (person)	el/la guía	ehl/lah **gee**-ah
guide (book)	la guía	lah **gee**-ah
map	el mapa	ehl **mah**-pah
taxi stand	sitio de taxis	**see**-tee-on deh **tahk**-sees

Staying in a Hotel

Do you have a vacant room?	¿Tienen una habitación libre?	tee-**eh**-nehn **oo**-nah ah-bee-tah-see-**ohn lee**-breh
double room	habitación doble	ah-bee-tah-see-**ohn doh**-bleh
single room	habitación sencilla	ah-bee-tah-see-**ohn** sehn-**see**-yah
room with a bath	habitación con baño	ah-bee-tah-see-**ohn** kohn **bah**-nyoh
shower	la ducha	lah **doo**-chah
I have a reservation	Tengo una habitación reservada	tehn-goh **oo**-nah ah-bee-tah-see-**ohn** reh-sehr-**vah**-dah
key	la llave	lah **yah**-veh

Eating Out

Have you got a table for…	¿Tienen mesa para…?	tee-**eh**-nehn meh-sah pah-**rah**
I want to reserve a table	Quiero reservar una mesa	kee-eh-roh reh-sehr-**vahr oo**-nah **meh**-sah
The bill, please	La cuenta, por favor	lah **kwehn**-tah pohr fah-**vohr**
I am a vegetarian	Soy vegetariano/a	soy veh-heh-tah-ree-**ah**-no/na
waiter/waitress	mesero/a	meh-**seh**-roh/rah
menu	la carta	lah **kahr**-tah
wine list	la carta de vinos	lah **kahr**-tah deh **vee**-nohs
glass	un vaso	oon **vah**-soh
bottle	una botella	**oo**-nah boh-**teh**-yah
knife	un cuchillo	oon koo-**chee**-yoh
fork	un tenedor	oon teh-neh-**dohr**
spoon	una cuchara	**oo**-nah koo-**chah**-rah
breakfast	el desayuno	ehl deh-sah-**yoo**-noh
lunch	la comida	lah koh-**mee**-dah
dinner	la cena	lah **seh**-nah
main course	el plato fuerte	ehl **plah**-toh foo-**ehr**-teh
starters	las entradas	lahs ehn-**trah**-das
dish of the day	el plato del día	ehl **plah**-toh dehl **dee**-ah
tip	la propina	lah proh-**pee**-nah
Is service included?	¿El servicio está incluido?	ehl sehr-**vee**-see-oh ehs-**tah** een-kloo-**ee**-doh

Menu Decoder

el aceite	ah-**see-eh**-teh	oil
las aceitunas	ah-seh-**toon**-ahs	olives
el agua mineral	**ah**-gwa mee-neh-**rahl**	mineral water
sin gas/con gas	seen gas/kohn gas	still/sparkling
el ajo	**ah**-hoh	garlic
el arroz	ahr-**rohs**	rice
el azúcar	ah-**soo**-kahr	sugar
la banana	bah-**nah**-nah	banana
una bebida	beh-**bee**-dah	drink
el café	kah-**feh**	coffee
la carne	**kahr**-neh	meat
la cebolla	seh-**boh**-yah	onion
la cerveza	sehr-**veh**-sah	beer
el cerdo	**sehr**-doh	pork
el chocolate	choh-koh-**lah**-teh	chocolate
la ensalada	ehn-sah-**lah**-dah	salad
la fruta	**froo**-tah	fruit
el helado	eh-**lah**-doh	ice cream
el huevo	oo-**eh**-voh	egg
el jugo	ehl **hoo**-goh	juice
la langosta	lahn-**gohs**-tah	lobster
la leche	**leh**-cheh	milk
la mantequilla	mahn-teh-**kee**-yah	butter
la manzana	mahn-**sah**-nah	apple
los mariscos	mah-**rees**-kohs	seafood
la naranja	nah-**rahn**-hah	orange
el pan	pahn	bread
las papas	**pah**-pahs	potatoes
el pescado	pehs-**kah**-doh	fish
picante	pee-**kahn**-teh	spicy
la pimienta	pee-mee-**yehn**-tah	pepper
el pollo	**poh**-yoh	chicken
el postre	**pohs**-treh	dessert
el queso	**keh**-soh	cheese
el refresco	reh-**frehs**-koh	soft drink/soda
la sal	sahl	salt
la salsa	**sahl**-sah	sauce
la sopa	**soh**-pah	soup
el té	teh	herb tea (usually camomile)
el té negro	teh neh-groh	tea
la torta	**tohr**-tah	sandwich
las tostadas	tohs-**tah**-dahs	toast
el vinagre	vee-**nah**-greh	vinegar
el vino blanco	**vee**-noh **blahn**-koh	white wine
el vino tinto	**vee**-noh **teen**-toh	red wine

Numbers

0	cero	**seh**-roh
1	uno	**oo**-noh
2	dos	dohs
3	tres	trehs
4	cuatro	**kwa**-troh
5	cinco	**seen**-koh
6	seis	says
7	siete	**see**-eh-teh
8	ocho	**oh**-choh
9	nueve	**nweh**-veh
10	diez	dee-**ehs**
11	once	**ohn**-seh
12	doce	**doh**-seh
13	trece	**treh**-seh
14	catorce	kah-**tohr**-seh
15	quince	**keen**-seh
16	dieciséis	dee-eh-see-**seh-ees**
17	diecisiete	dee-eh-see-see-**eh**-teh
18	dieciocho	dee-eh-see-**oh**-choh
19	diecinueve	dee-eh-see-**nweh**-veh
20	veinte	**veh**-een-teh
21	veintiuno	veh-een-tee-**oo**-noh
22	veintidós	veh-een-tee-**dohs**
30	treinta	**treh**-een-tah
31	treinta y uno	treh-een-tah ee **oo**-noh
40	cuarenta	kwah-**rehn**-tah
50	cincuenta	seen-**kwehn**-tah
60	sesenta	seh-**sehn**-tah
70	setenta	seh-**tehn**-tah
80	ochenta	oh-**chehn**-tah
90	noventa	noh-**vehn**-tah
100	cien	see-**ehn**
101	ciento uno	see-**ehn**-toh **oo**-noh
102	ciento dos	see-**ehn**-toh dohs
200	doscientos	dohs-see-**ehn**-tohs
500	quinientos	khee-nee-**ehn**-tohs
700	setecientos	seh-teh-see-**ehn**-tohs
900	novecientos	noh-veh-see-**ehn**-tohs
1,000	mil	meel
1,001	mil uno	meel **oo**-noh

Time

one minute	un minuto	**oon** mee-**noo**-toh
one hour	una hora	**oo**-nah **oh**-rah
half an hour	media hora	**meh**-dee-ah **oh**-rah
half past one	la una y media	lah **oo**-nah ee **meh**-dee-ah
Monday	lunes	**loo**-nehs
Tuesday	martes	**mahr**-tehs
Wednesday	miércoles	mee-**ehr**-koh-lehs
Thursday	jueves	hoo-**weh**-vehs
Friday	viernes	vee-**ehr**-nehs
Saturday	sábado	**sah**-bah-doh
Sunday	domingo	doh-**meen**-goh